The Imagist Poem

The Imagist Poem:
Modern Poetry In Miniature

Revised Edition by
William Pratt

Story Line Press
Ashland, Oregon

Published by Story Line Press, Three Oaks Farms, PO Box 1240, Ashland, OR 97520-0055
www.storylinepress.com

ISBN: 1-58654-009-2
Book design by Lysa McDowell
Cover design by Paul Davis

Library of Congress Cataloging-in-Publication Data

The imagist poem : modern poetry in miniature/[edited by] William Pratt.—Rev. ed.
        p. cm.
    Includes bibliographical references.
    ISBN 1-58654-009-2
    1. Imagist poetry. 2. American poetry—20th century. 3. English poetry—20th century.
    I. Pratt, William, 1927–

PS614 .I43 2001b
811'.520811—dc21

                                                                2001049340

Acknowledgments:

For computer assistance in revising this anthology, I wish to thank my son, William Stuart Pratt, Data Base Analyst for IBM, Burlington, Vermont.

For editorial suggestions, I am in debt to John Gery, Research Professor of English, University of New Orleans, Louisiana.

Grateful acknowledgment is also made to the following for permission to quote from copyright material:

H.D.: "Helen" and "Hymn," reprinted from *H.D.: Selected Poems* by permission of the publishers, Grove Press, Inc. Copyright 1957 by Norman Holmes Pearson. Reprinted by permission of New Directions Publishing Corp.

WILLIAM CARLOS WILLIAMS: "The Locust Tree in Flower," "Flowers by the Sea," "Nantucket," "Bird," reprinted from *The Collected Earlier Poems of William Carlos Williams* by permission of New Directions, Publishers. Copyright 1938, 1951 by William Carlos Williams. "Iris," "Landscape with the Fall of Icarus," "A Sort of a Song" reprinted from *Pictures from Brueghel* by William Carlos Williams by permission of New Directions Publishers. Copyright 1962 by William Carlos Williams.

D. H. LAWRENCE: "Trees in the Garden," "Swan" and "November by the Sea" reprinted from *The Complete Poems of D. H. Lawrence* by permission of Viking Penguin, a division of Penguin Putnam, Inc.

MARIANNE MOORE: "A Talisman" from *Observations*, Copyright 1924 by Marianne Moore. "To a Chameleon," Copyright 1954 by Marianne Moore, from *The Complete Poems of Marianne Moore*. Used by permission of Viking Penguin, a division of Penguin Putnam Inc. "The Fish" and "No Swan So Fine" by Marianne Moore. Reprinted with the permission of Scribner, a division of Simon & Schuster, from *The Collected Poems of Marianne Moore*. Copyright 1935 by Marianne Moore; copyright renewed 1963 by Marianne Moore and T.S. Eliot.

WALLACE STEVENS: "Study of Two Pears" by Wallace Stevens, from *Collected Poems* by Wallace Stevens. Copyright 1942 by Wallace Stevens and renewed 1970 by Holly Stevens. Reprinted by permission of Alfred A. Knopf, a division of Random House Inc. "Farewell Without a Guitar" by Wallace Stevens, from *Collected Poems* by Wallace Stevens. Copyright 1957 by Elsie Stevens and Holly Stevens. Reprinted by permission of Alfred A. Knopf, a division of Random House Inc.

E. E. CUMMINGS: "l(a" Copyright 1958, 1986, 1991 by the Trustees for the E. E. Cummings Trust, from *Complete Poems 1904-1962* by E. E. Cummings, edited by George J. Firmage. Used by permission of Liveright Publishing Corporation.

ARCHIBALD MACLEISH: "Ars Poetica" from *Collected Poems by Archibald MacLeish 1917-1982* by Archibald MacLeish. Copyright 1985 by The Estate of Archibald MacLeish. Reprinted by permission of Houghton Mifflin Company. All rights reserved.

For Ezra Pound, If He Wants It

Preface to the Original Edition

This collection of the first "modern" poems in English hopes to satisfy several needs:

1) to provide an introduction, and if possible an access, to contemporary poetry by the most direct means available: the short experimental poems with which it began;
2) to define the Imagist poem as a literary type, in theory and in practice, and to demonstrate the scope of its achievement within the larger whole of modern poetry;
3) to set down, as a matter of record, what has proved to be the most original poetic movement of the twentieth century, so that it can be better understood both as it succeeded and as it failed;
4) to offer a collection of some of the finest short poems in modern English, simply for the reader's pleasure and delight.

In choosing each poem for this anthology, some admittedly arbitrary, but reasonably consistent, principles have been applied:
a) centrality to the period when Imagism was in flower, from 1908 to 1917; b) similarity to poems published at that time, whether by other poets in the period immediately following, or by Imagist poets at a later date. Ultimately, each entry has been chosen because of its value as a separate poem, regardless of whether it could definitely be labeled as "Imagist." Some of the choices are bound to seem more arbitrary than others, and the only justification for them is that, in the end, it seemed impossible to exclude them.

WILLIAM PRATT

1963

Preface to the Revised Edition

The first edition of this anthology appeared shortly after the middle of the twentieth century, when the Imagists were rapidly fading into history. It stayed in print for about twenty years, and then was out of print for almost twenty more, and now this second edition is appearing at the beginning of the twenty-first century, when the Imagists are widely recognized as the initiators of some of the best Twentieth Century poetry. Thus the poetic movement with which "Modernism" began, early in the last century, takes on new credibility at the beginning of another century. That the Imagists are the most important poetic school to emerge in the English-speaking world since the Romantics is now a fact of literary history, and there is no longer any need to withhold the full credit they deserve as reinvigorators of an already rich poetic tradition.

Imagism emerged, during the second decade of the Twentieth Century, from a welter of competing and mostly short-lived artistic fads, with strange names like Futurism, Dadaism, Cubism, Vorticism—even a hoax called Spectrism with spurious principles and artfully contrived poems—to become the mainstream of the Modernist movement in literature. Like other fads, Imagism was derided by some and dismissed by others. Yet it persisted. Why? The main reason was that it brought together several poets who proved to be major, notably Ezra Pound, H.D., William Carlos Williams, and D.H. Lawrence, all of whom were practicing a new poetic form. The only other artistic movement that was as long-lasting was Cubism, whose major artists were Picasso and Braque. But Cubism was never put into writing: it consisted entirely of paintings, and was strictly a visual technique for other painters to follow, none of whom were as gifted as Picasso and Braque. Imagism not only had formidable poets, but had its do's and its don'ts, appealed to a number of talented followers, and produced some genuine new poems (the *Spectra Hoax* was amusing, but it was all parodies, and quickly became dated). Imagism provided models for artistic experimentation, as did Cubism, but at the same time it stressed some fundamentals of poetic form, such as imagery, brevity, and free verse. That Imagism developed suddenly and somewhat haphazardly among a few young and ambitious English and American poets only confirms its essential rightness. By stating some perennially valid principles of poetry, and appealing to a wide range of talents beyond the original group, it was able to gather momentum through artistic imitation, and in time it embraced many of the poets we now recognize as major Modernists: not simply Pound and H.D. and Williams and Lawrence, who were associated with the Imagists early in their careers, but others who were not, such as Eliot and Stevens and Moore and Cummings and MacLeish. There were minor as well as major Imagists throughout the Imagist decade, but the influence spread primarily from the major figures. Together, Imagist theory and practice defined a new poetic style.

The new poetic style gave Modernism its start early in the twentieth century; it also gave new definition to poetry written much earlier. The Imagists, taking Pound at his word to "Make it New," opened the way for radical experiments in poetic technique, helping readers understand what earlier poets like Emily Dickinson and Stephen Crane had been doing decades earlier. They had seemed isolated figures in the late nineteenth century, and even had trouble getting their new kinds of poems published, but when, in the early twentieth century, the Imagists made short poems in free verse the norm, Dickinson and Crane seemed ahead of their time. These two American originals were largely unappreciated in their day, but now both Dickinson and Crane can be seen as "Pre-Imagists," anticipating the poetic style to come. Similarly, there are later poets who might qualify as "Post-Imagists" or "Neo-Imagists" (though none of them are as distinctive as Dickinson or Crane), since they went on writing the sort of short free verse poems first popularized by the Imagists. More importantly, the later poetry of Pound and Williams and Lawrence and Stevens and Moore and Cummings bears witness to Imagist principles. Looking both backward and forward in literary history, it is clearer now than it was forty years ago, when this anthology first appeared, that Anglo-American Imagism, which started as an avant garde movement in the wake of French Symbolism, was the wellspring out of which the main current of Modernism in English flowed.

WILLIAM PRATT

2001

11

Contents

T. S. ELIOT:

AMY LOWELL:

JOHN GOULD FLETCHER:

Note: The Introduction is substantially the same as in the original edition, with only minor changes in the wording and a few added footnotes to bring it up to date, but one poet and thirteen poems have been added to the Contents—most notably T.S. Eliot, whose four early "Preludes" and "Morning at the Window" might well have been in the first edition—and several later items have been added to the Bibliography as well.

Introduction

PART I. THE ORIGINALITY OF THE IMAGIST POEM

It remains a strange but striking fact that the creative moment of modern poetry coincided with the destructive moment of modern history. For it was during the decade between 1910 and 1920, when the First World War was being fought in Europe, that the battle for a new poetic style was being fought in England and America. From this creative-destructive process came, in time, such masterpieces as the later poetry of Yeats and the longer poems of Pound and Eliot, culminating in *The Waste Land*, that nightmare of the imagination from which we have never quite succeeded in waking up. There is no doubt that the major works of modern English poetry contain much of the destructiveness prevalent then—and since—in our civilization, but it is worth remembering that they came out of a period of poetic activity which had much that was creative about it, when a literary movement flourished and a series of minor masterpieces were produced. This was the Imagist decade, and its product was the Imagist poem.

The Imagist poem was the invention of a small group of English and American poets who worked together in London during the first and second decades of this century, but for formal models it reached far back into the past and into languages other than English, and for contributors it was not confined to any of the groups (and there was more than one) who called themselves "Imagist." The Imagist poem was a hybrid, and being a hybrid it throve by a process of continual cross-fertilization. Like the sonnet and blank verse of Shakespeare's time, which were the standard forms of English poetry from the late sixteenth until the early twentieth century, the Imagist poem was produced by the grafting of poetic forms from other languages onto English. The sonnet and blank verse came, as we know, from the root stock of Italian and Latin poetry (chiefly through Wyatt's translation of Petrarchan sonnets and Surrey's translation of the *Aeneid*), and almost every English poet of the Elizabethan Age formed his poetic style by writing sonnets. The modern English poet ranged much farther afield in seeking his new style—the Imagists adapted from ancient Chinese, classical Greek, and contemporary French Symbolist poems, in turn—but in time almost every important poet tried his hand at something like the Imagist poem. Eliot's "Preludes" are only the most eminent example of the kind of poem which many poets produced at the time of the Imagist experiments, whether or not consciously under their influence. Although Eliot himself was not officially an Imagist, it was he who confirmed the historical importance of the movement when he said that "The point de repère usually and conveniently taken, as the starting-point of modern poetry, is the group denominated ...'imagist' in London about 1910. I was not there."[1] This was his acknowledgment that modern English poetry originated in a common effort, by a number of individual talents, to revitalize English verse. Just as the sonnet-sequences of the late sixteenth century were the prelude to the mature works of Spenser, Sidney, and Shakespeare, and other accomplished poets of that day, so the hundreds of Imagist poems that were produced early in the twentieth century were the prelude to mature works as diverse as those of Pound and Eliot, Wallace Stevens and Marianne Moore, William Carlos Williams and D. H. Lawrence, Archibald MacLeish and E. E. Cummings. The words which T. E. Hulme wrote at the beginning of the Imagist movement must seem peculiarly prophetic now:

A particular convention or attitude in art has a strict analogy to the phenomena of organic life. It grows old and decays. It has a definite period of life and must die. All the possible tunes get played on it and then it is exhausted; moreover its best period is its youngest. Take the case of the extraordinary efflorescence of verse in the Elizabethan period. All kinds of reasons have been given for

[1] Eliot, "American Literature and the American Language" in *To Criticize the Critic* (New York: Farrar, Straus & Giroux, 1965), 58.

this—the discovery of the new world and the rest of it. There is a much simpler one. A new medium had been given them to play with—namely, blank verse. It was new and so it was easy to play new tunes on it.[2]

If the Imagist poem is a more flexible form than the Elizabethan sonnet, just as "free verse" is a more flexible form than "blank verse," the fact may be a measure of the greater uncertainty, the deeper spiritual unrest, of our time in comparison with that of the Elizabethans. But there is no doubt that Imagism was the means by which most of the masters of modern English verse discovered their own style, and in some sense every important poet of the twentieth century was an Imagist, just as every important poet of the seventeenth century was a sonneteer.

If so, then the originality of Imagism need hardly be questioned, for, at the very least, it is a name which connects many of the major poetic talents of the present century. But it is also a name for a poetic form and a set of poetic theories which are basic to modern poetry in English. And, as is often overlooked, it is the name for a number of the finest short poems written in the twentieth century, poems as different as Sandburg's "Fog" and MacLeish's "Ars Poetica," Williams' "The Red Wheelbarrow" and Pound's "The Return." Because there was no earlier volume in which all the best poems of the Imagist type appeared together, there was no previous opportunity to see what the range of the Imagist poem was, nor to recognize that its originality was something more than a name and a fashion. This anthology, by combining for the first time the history, theory, and practice of a brief but decisive literary movement, demonstrated convincingly that the Imagist poem was both a beginning and an achievement: that, taken as a whole, it is modern poetry in miniature.

PART II. THE HISTORY OF THE IMAGIST POEM

René Taupin, who was the first to make a serious study of the Imagist period in American poetry, *The Influence of French Symbolism on Modern American Poetry*, remarked with French

---

[2] Hulme, "Romanticism and Classicism," in *Speculations*, ed. Herbert Read (New York: Harcourt, Brace, 1924), 121-22.

precision: "It is more accurate to consider Imagism not as a doctrine, nor even as a poetic school, but as the association of a few poets who were for a certain time—a matter of weeks rather than of months—in agreement on a small number of important principles."[3] It would perhaps be best to say of the history of the Imagist movement that it consisted of a succession of "creative moments" rather than of any continuous or sustained period of development. Like those moments of "real time" during which evolutionary changes occur, according to the philosophy of Henri Bergson (under whom T. E. Hulme studied for a time), the periods of Imagist activity were brief, sporadic, and practically discontinuous. Which is only to say that the history of Imagism was like its poetic product—a pattern of lucid intervals.

1. The School of Images, 1908-09

The first of these intervals occurred in the years 1908-09 in London, when a headstrong young Englishman named T. E. Hulme, freshly expelled from Cambridge for participating in a tavern brawl, collected around him a group of restless young writers, who first formed themselves into a Poets' Club, and then dissolved and re-formed into what one of the members, Ezra Pound, looked back on in 1912 as "the forgotten School of Images." The name suits the whole first period of Imagism, because it was much more like a "school" than the later periods, and because Hulme was so obviously its first schoolmaster. Very little poetry of the Imagist sort was written during this time—in fact, out of all that the Poets' Club produced, only Hulme's poem "Autumn" (which appeared in a small pamphlet of poems called *Christmas 1908*) seems now to deserve the name of "Imagist," and it was an example too isolated to be of any importance until a few years later. But the dissatisfaction with current English poetry and the experiment with new forms had begun in earnest, and was continued into the following year, when Hulme was brought into contact first with F. S. Flint, a fellow Englishman, and then with Ezra Pound, an American newly arrived in London.

3 Taupin, *The Influence of French Symbolism on Modern American Poetry*, translated by William Pratt and Anne Rich Pratt (New York: AMS Press, 1985), 116.

In a "History of Imagism" written for the *Egoist* magazine in 1915,[4] Flint described the activities of this new group, the successors to the Poets' Club, which began its meetings in a Soho restaurant in the spring of 1909.[5] He said that the first meeting, in March, included Hulme, Flint, Edward Storer, F. W. Tancred, Joseph Campbell, and Florence Farr, and that Pound appeared for the first time at an April meeting, introduced by Miss Farr and a friend of Flint's named T. D. Fitzgerald. At these meetings, most of the talk evidently centered on poetic technique, and a variety of foreign verse forms were discussed, from the vers libre of the recent French Symbolists to the older Japanese tanka and haiku, and from what Flint called "a sacred Hebrew form, of which 'This is the house that Jack built' is a perfect model," to the Provençal troubador songs which Pound so much admired, and which appear to have been his main contribution to the discussion. According to Flint's account, it was Hulme who insisted always upon "absolutely accurate presentation and no verbiage," and who would "spend hours each day in the search for the right phrase." And, as Flint put it, "There was also a lot of talk and practice among us, Storer leading it chiefly, of what we called the Image."

In Flint's opinion—and he forms the only real connecting link between the three main periods of Imagism—Edward Storer was the first to publish a book of Imagist poems, but the claim seems somewhat exaggerated now. At any rate, the one poem Flint quoted as an example of Storer's Imagism:

Forsaken lovers
Burning to a chaste white moon,
Upon strange pyres of loneliness and drought.

though it was titled "Image," and though it was in a free verse form, seems in retrospect more late-Romantic than Imagist both in subject and sentiment.

The "School of Images" was important more for its theorizing than for its practical poetic achievement: neither the Imagist name nor anything definite in Imagist form was to emerge until a few

---

4 Actually, although the article was signed by Flint, much of it was paraphrased directly from an interview with Pound. See "Documents on Imagism from the Papers of F.S. Flint" by Christopher Middleton, the *The Review* (London) no. 15 (April, 1965), 35–51.

5 A more detailed account of these meetings may be found in an article by A.R. Jones, biographer of Hulme. See "Notes Toward a History of Imagism," *South Atlantic Quarterly*, LX (Summer, 1961), pp. 262-85.

years later. The group gradually dissolved during the winter of 1909, and nothing more was heard from it until, in November of 1912, Ezra Pound published a book of his own poems called *Ripostes*, and to it attached an appendix called "The Complete Poetical Works of T. E. Hulme," consisting of five short poems, of which the first was "Autumn." In his explanatory note, Pound mentioned "'the School of Images,' which may or may not have existed," and used for the first time the word "Imagiste" (spelling it with a characteristic French flourish) to describe a new group of poets formed only a short time earlier. "As for the future," he said in his note, "Les Imagistes, the descendants of the forgotten school of 1909, have that in their keeping." Who these Imagistes were, Pound neglected to say, but he appears to have been thinking mainly of three: H.D. (a pen-name Pound invented for Hilda Doolittle, an American with whom he had had a romance in Philadelphia, before coming to London), Richard Aldington (a young Englishman, later married to H.D. for a short time), and himself. Hulme was not a member of the new group, but Pound was acknowledging its debt to him as the leader of the initial movement, and giving his poems prominence as examples of the new Imagism.

2. Les Imagistes, 1912-14

Actually, however, it was not Hulme but H.D. who had provided Pound with the direct inspiration for the new school of "Imagistes." Judging from Pound's letters, it must have been during October of 1912, in the British Museum Tea Room, that H.D. showed him a group of poems which, when he sent them to Harriet Monroe for publication in the newly founded *Poetry* magazine in Chicago, he described as being "in the laconic speech of the Imagistes, even if the subject is classic." These poems were published in the January, 1913, issue of *Poetry*; they were "Hermes of the Ways," "Priapus" (later retitled "Orchard"), and "Epigram." These, together with the short "Oread," that appeared early the next year in the *Egoist*, were the defining works of the second, decisive phase of Imagism. H.D.'s poems were of a higher poetic refinement than Hulme's, combining a notable simplicity of diction with an irregular but distinctly musical cadence that derived from her discipline in the classical Greek lyric. Pound was so struck by the clarity and intensity of these poems, by their "hardness," as he liked to call it, that he afterward declared that Imagism had been founded in order to publicize them.[6]

But important as H.D.'s poems were to the new movement, they were not the whole of it. Pound's own poetry, after many refinements, had been arriving at a new precision of form and new concision of statement: his "Doria," modeled on the Greek lyric, and "The Return," modeled on a French Symbolist poem, had appeared in *Ripostes*, and in the next two years he was to publish a number of other poems of the Imagist type, including some that were modeled on the Japanese haiku form, of which "In a Station of the Metro" is the best known. Richard Aldington was also publishing short, free verse poems at this time, as was F. S. Flint, and both had their effect on the shaping of the new medium. Most important of all, in giving the name a definite meaning, were the two brief essays which appeared in the March, 1913, issue of *Poetry*: one by Flint, entitled "Imagisme," and the other by Pound, called "A Few Don'ts by an Imagiste." These essays represented the first serious attempt at a statement of Imagist principles.

Evidently such a statement was needed, for Harriet Monroe, who had first mentioned the name "Imagist" in the second issue of her magazine, announced in her accompanying Editor's Note:

In response to many requests for information regarding Imagism and the Imagistes, we publish this note by Mr. Flint, supplementing it with further exemplification by Mr. Pound. It will be seen from these that Imagism is not necessarily associated with Hellenic subjects, or with vers libre as a prescribed form.

Flint's statement began by protesting that the Imagists "were not a revolutionary school; their only endeavor was to write in accordance with the best tradition, as they found it in the best writers of all time,—in Sappho, Catullus, Villon." But he went on to give three rules which were not found in any previous literary tradition, and which the Imagists applied to the writing of their poetry:

---

[6] See H.D.'s account in *End to Torment: A Memoir of Ezra Pound* (New York: New Directions, 1979), 18.

1. Direct treatment of the "thing" whether subjective or objective.

2. To use absolutely no word that does not contribute to the presentation.

As regarding rhythm: to compose in the sequence of the musical phrase, not in sequence of a metronome.

As a fourth rule, Flint referred enigmatically to "a certain 'Doctrine of the Image,' which they had not committed to writing; they said that it did not concern the public, and would provoke useless discussion." Pound, however, resolved some of the enigma by providing, along with his "Don'ts," a one-sentence definition: "An 'Image' is that which presents an intellectual and emotional complex in an instant of time." He clarified it by adding, "It is the presentation of such a 'complex' instantaneously which gives the sense of sudden liberation; that sense of freedom from time limits and space limits; that sense of sudden growth, which we experience in the presence of the greatest works of art." And he emphasized its importance by declaring, "It is better to present one Image in a lifetime than to produce voluminous works."

These three rules, together with the definition, helped to dispel the clouds of mystery that had hung about the word "Imagism." Their effect was to suggest that, if Imagism was a club, it was a club which others might join. And in the pages of *Poetry* during the following months, an astonishing number of American poets showed their eagerness to join by contributing poems in the Imagist style. But the headquarters of Imagism was still in London, and the English influence of the Imagists was extended by means of a new magazine, the *Egoist*, which started publication in January of 1914, with Pound and Aldington as its literary editors. In its pages, in the next few months, appeared Imagist poems by Flint, Aldington, Pound, H.D., Amy Lowell, John Gould Fletcher, William Carlos Williams, D. H. Lawrence—and by many other aspiring poets who were caught up in the new movement toward freer expression. By the spring of 1914, when the first anthology of Imagism was published, the movement was already well launched and sailing, it seemed, toward the open sea.

This first anthology, edited by Pound and bearing the French title, *Des Imagistes*, included most of the names that were by then associated with Imagism, and a number of others besides. There were eleven poets in all, four of them charter members—Aldington, H.D., Flint, and Pound—and the others new initiates—Amy Lowell, William Carlos Williams, Skipwith Cannell, Allen Upward, and John Cournos, as well as two then relatively unknown prose writers— James Joyce and Ford Madox Hueffer (who had not yet changed his last name to Ford). The thirty-odd poems in the volume were of a mixed quality of excellence, and were written in a variety of poetic forms, from prose to rhymed and metered verse, but all were quite short, were prevailingly in free verse and informal diction, and bore the stamp of three main poetic influences: the classical Greek lyric, the Japanese haiku, and recent French Symbolist poetry of the vers libre type. But other than being the products of a highly literate group, these poems had less in common than might have been expected, and it seems obvious that Pound as editor was trying less to restrict Imagism than to extend it to include all the writers he respected. In this aim, however, he was opposed by some of the original group, especially by Aldington, who felt that Imagism was already too inclusive, and by Amy Lowell, who argued for a more democratic management and hoped to do some promoting of her own. When she began making arrangements with an American publisher to bring out an annual Imagist anthology, of a character more of her own choosing, she abruptly ended the second period of Imagism. Her letter to Pound, inviting him to join a reformed Imagist group in which a majority vote would determine selection, touched off a war of words which resulted in an immediate victory for Miss Lowell (though it may seem, looking back, in an ultimate victory for Pound).

3. The "Amygists," 1915-17

It would perhaps be fairest to both sides to say that at the crucial stage of Imagist development one master propagandist was vanquished by another. The pity is that the master propagandist who won was a less gifted poet than the one who lost. The final stage of Imagism, therefore, though its influence continued to expand and its unofficial membership to grow, was somewhat less promising than the earlier stages. Something may have been gained by setting a limit of six contributors to the three annual volumes, thereby insuring a more uniform quality, but something was also lost, and that something was the sense of a vital, emergent form. Pound is reported to have said, after his first meeting with Amy Lowell, "When I get through with that girl she'll think she was born in free verse," but the result was that she became too free with it, and even the best of her poems, read now, betray a limited musical sense. Moreover, the poems in the three anthologies she was responsible for tended toward greater and greater length—even H.D. became wordier, after the initial volume—and in time the clear outline of the Imagist poem, its terse and sculptured form, became blurred. This was an inevitable development, no doubt, for the poetry of Pound and of other experimenters with the Imagist form was also expanding at the same time, but the result of such changes in poems clearly marked "Imagist" was confusion rather than clarity. It was the fate of the later Imagist anthologies to record the fact that, as William Carlos Williams afterward put it, "Imagism failed because it lost structural necessity." To all outward signs, however, Imagism was flourishing during this third and final period. Imagist poems were appearing everywhere—in *Poetry* and in the newly established *Little Review*, both in Chicago, and in the *Egoist* in London. In May, 1915, the *Egoist* published a "Special Imagist Number," and as late as 1918, the *Little Review* ran a Vers Libre contest, which had a number of entries, and was won by a characteristic Imagist poem by H.D. But the final stage of Imagism—or "Amygism," as Pound wryly nicknamed it—is best represented by the three anthologies published, according to Amy Lowell's arrangement, by Houghton, Mifflin of Boston in 1915, 1916, and 1917. All were titled *Some Imagist Poets,* a title which was simply a translation of Pound's earlier French title, and accurate enough, since four of the six contributors had been included in Pound's first anthology: Aldington, H.D., Flint, and Amy Lowell herself. The two new members were equally well known, though their association with Imagism was of more recent date; they were the American poet, John Gould Fletcher, an early expatriate, and the rising English poet and novelist, D. H. Lawrence. Pound had spoken well of both poets before, but had not included them in the first Imagist anthology for reasons of his own. Of the six, H.D. was still the most perfect craftsman, but Lawrence, whose poetic style was by then well developed, was clearly the most creative influence. Lawrence, however, gained at least as much from his association with Imagism as he gave to it. His natural style was often repetitious and verbose, and frequently moralizing (no doubt legacies from Whitman, whom of all poets he most resembles), but those poems in which he came nearest to achieving the Imagist concentration are among his finest. That some of them—like the dazzling "November by the Sea"—are also among his last, shows how instinctive the Imagist treatment became with him in time.

Of the three later Imagist volumes, the first one, published in 1915, was highest in poetic quality and most consistently Imagist in form. There was somewhat less variety, and less conciseness, than in the poems of Pound's anthology, but the poetic level was high and the Imagist rules were largely observed. In fact, these rules were restated and redefined in the Preface, to make even clearer the principles which these poets stood for. The original three rules were expanded to six, and considerably amplified:

1. To use the language of common speech, but to employ always the exact word, not the nearly-exact, nor the merely decorative word.

2. To create new rhythms—as the expression of new moods—and not to copy old rhythms, which merely echo old moods. We do not insist upon "free-verse" as the only method of writing poetry. We fight for it as a principle of liberty. We believe that the individuality of a poet may often be better expressed in free-verse than in conventional forms. In poetry, a new cadence means a new idea.

3. To allow absolute freedom in the choice of subject. It is not good art to write badly about aeroplanes and automobiles; nor is it necessarily bad art to write well about the past. We believe passionately in the artistic value of modern life, but we wish to point out that there is nothing so uninspiring nor so old-fashioned as an aeroplane of the year 1911.

4. To present an image (hence the name: "Imagist"). We are not a school of painters, but we believe that poetry should render particulars exactly and not deal in vague generalities, however magnificent and sonorous. It is for this reason that we oppose the cosmic poet, who seems to us to shirk the real difficulties of his art.

5. To produce poetry that is hard and clear, never blurred nor indefinite.

6. Finally, most of us believe that concentration is of the very essence of poetry.

If these principles added no new idea to the original Imagist platform, they at least helped to clarify it. Even Pound, who later maintained that the "Amygists" had erred by ignoring the second Imagist principle ("To use absolutely no word that does not contribute to the presentation"), could hardly have objected to their principles. If the second and third Imagist anthologies had maintained the principles as consistently as the first one did, then Imagism might have attained a new kind of clarity in its final period of development. However the volumes of 1916 and 1917 reflected less the common principles than the different styles of the six contributors: Amy Lowell's "Patterns," H.D.'s "Eurydice," and Lawrence's "Terra Nuova" (or "New Heaven and Earth"), though excellent in themselves, were rather far from the Imagist doctrines of concentration and economy. In fact, it may be said that these poems prove the limitations of the strict Imagist form: for poets who had once found it suited to their development, it was now too restrictive; without abandoning the Imagist experiments, they were reaching out for a more extensive vehicle to carry the weight of their meaning.

After 1917, then, Imagism was no longer a movement: it had become a tool, which each poet could adapt to his own use. Younger poets like E. E. Cummings and Archibald MacLeish would make new poems of the Imagist type, but without forming any association or publishing further rules, though MacLeish's famous "Ars Poetica" could well serve as the poetic definition— and epitaph—of the whole Imagist movement. Older poets, who had already forged their weapons in the Imagist fire, would use them to fight bigger wars than the strict Imagist poem permitted. But some of them would return to it much later on and use it as Wallace Stevens did in such poems as "Farewell Without a Guitar," to distill the meaning of a lifetime into a single drop. In such a poem (and there are other later examples in this collection) the value of the Imagist experiments of 1910-20 is once again confirmed, and the Imagist form, in all its concentration and brilliance, is given new life.

PART III. THE THEORY OF THE IMAGIST POEM

Though it is possible to speak with some justice of an "Imagist form," any history of the movement makes it clear that this form was never fixed. The whole force of Imagism was in the direction of variety, irregularity, and individuality, for it had begun as a protest against the rigidity of traditional English verse forms, and it continually sought new models to imitate and transform, never settling permanently on any one of them. Not since the Elizabethans had English poetry been subjected to such a variety of foreign influences, nor had the cadence of English verse been so radically altered. What emerged from the Imagist experiments was not nearly so definite a thing as the Elizabethan sonnet or blank verse line; yet, unmistakably, a form had been impressed upon English poetry which had never been there before. Somehow, out of the wildly eclectic borrowings from Oriental, classical, medieval, and modern sources, a new cadence had come into English verse—"free verse," it was called; and out of a few intuitive principles had come a new sense of metaphor—"Imagism," a fresh perception of the relation of language to meaning.

The nature of this change was first defined in a lecture on "modern" poetry which T. E. Hulme gave to the group that formed the first "School of Images." He suggested that "modern" art, as it was then emerging, was different from the art of the past in that "it no longer deals with heroic action, it has become definitely and finally introspective and deals with expression and communication of momentary phases in the poet's mind."[7] He explained that the "mystery of things" was no longer perceived as "action" but instead as "impression," and predicted that "What has found expression in painting as impressionism will soon find expression in poetry as free verse." The analogy was apt, as Hulme's analogies so often were, and the prediction was remarkably far-sighted. The techniques of the French Impressionist painters, out of which the whole of modern painting sprang, were the product of the same kind of inner experience that gave rise to the vers libre of the French Symbolist poets, at about the same historical moment—and

---

[7] Hulme, "A Lecture on Modern Poetry," in *Further Speculations*, ed. Sam Hynes (Minneapolis: University of Minnesota Press, 1955), 68.

also, if Hulme had cared to add them, to the psychological novels of Flaubert, Henry James, and Joseph Conrad. Hulme did not add them, because he was primarily interested in poetry rather than in prose. ("Prose a museum where all the old weapons of poetry kept"[8] was typical of his notes.) What he meant was that poetic techniques should become subtle enough to record exactly the momentary impressions—the images, as he liked to call them— which were the real substance of experience.

1. Free Verse

"Free verse" is a term which is so often misused as to need redefinition each time it is mentioned. But there is no mistaking the fact that for Hulme, as for Flint and Pound, free verse meant form— not formlessness. In one of his essays on Bergson's philosophy, Hulme spoke scornfully of "the people who dream of the glorious kind of new poetry that would arise if inspiration could only be emancipated from the hampering restrictions of rhyme, metre, and form generally,"[9] and went on to explain, by an analogy from animal evolution, that the shape of a bird came not merely from its desire to fly, but from its having to fly in air against the force of gravity. Though he was only occasionally a practicing poet, Hulme understood that poetry could not exist without a definite form; but he felt that poetic form should respond more directly to the inner control of the impression, or image, than to the outer control of a pre-established pattern of accent and rhyme. He believed that it was harder to write poems in this kind of organic, or natural, form than in a traditional verse form, for in his early lecture he declared that "It is a delicate and difficult art, that of evoking an image, of fitting the rhythm to the idea, and one is tempted to fall back to the comforting and easy arms of the old, regular metre, which takes away all the trouble for us."[10]

In the decade following Hulme's lecture, free verse became so much a trademark of Imagist poetry that it was necessary for Amy Lowell's group, in the first of its anthologies, to demur, "We do not

---

[8] Hulme, "Notes on Language and Style," *Further Speculations*, 81.

[9] Hulme, "Notes on Bergson," *Further Speculations*, 60.

[10]Hulme, "Lecture on Modern Poetry," *Further Speculations*, 74.

insist upon 'free-verse' as the only method of writing poetry." By that time, there was more evidence of freedom than of verse in many of the experiments, until T. S. Eliot felt impelled to protest that "No vers is libre for the man who wants to do a good job." However, the principle of free verse as it was formulated in the first set of Imagist rules—"As regarding rhythm: to compose in the sequence of the musical phrase, not in sequence of a metronome"—and as it was exemplified in the best Imagist poems (especially those of H.D. and Pound) was quite sound, and led far beyond the Imagist movement proper, into the major developments of modern poetry. Free verse is still difficult to define, even after a century in which it has been the dominant poetic mode, but it may best be understood as being more closely allied to music than to prose or to direct speech—at any rate, such an understanding will help to distinguish the free verse of the Imagists from that of such precursors as Whitman or Stephen Crane, who are often thought of as the inventors of free verse in English. Free verse, in the broad sense of poetry composed of unrhymed, irregular lines ("cadence," as Flint liked to call it), was not new with the Imagists, nor with Crane or Whitman; it went back at least as far as Milton and *Samson Agonistes*; but with the Imagists, free verse for the first time became a discipline and acquired status as a legitimate poetic form. As Herbert Read put it, speaking of the most influential Imagist poet: "Pound did not invent free verse—he reformed free verse, gave it a musical structure, and to that extent we may say paradoxically that it was no longer free."[11]

Pound, besides contributing to the practice of free verse, contributed also to its theory, especially in his notion of "absolute rhythm." In 1912, in an essay which appeared in Harold Monro's *Poetry and Drama* magazine, Pound asserted: "I believe in an 'absolute rhythm,' a rhythm, that is, in poetry which corresponds exactly to the emotion or shade of emotion to be expressed." And later on, in 1914, in an essay on "Vorticism" that appeared in the *Fortnightly Review*, Pound said that this belief in "absolute rhythm" led to vers libre and to experiments in "quantitative verse." He obviously meant that "absolute rhythm" and "free verse" were not contradictory but equivalent terms, poetry being "freest" when most expressive, when rhythm and meaning seem to move together as one. In the Imagist poem the rhythm was "chosen" to fit the subject

---

[11]Read, "Ezra Pound," in *The Tenth Muse* (London: Routledge & Kegan Paul, 1957), 264-65.

just as the words were chosen; every true poem should have its own inner order, and the only real "freedom" was in the subject—the image—with which the poem began.

2. The Image

What, then, is the image of an Imagist poem? The term is as difficult to define as that of free verse. Images and imagery existed in poetry long before "Imagism" did, and this fact led some unsympathetic critics to say that the Imagists were merely dressing up old ideas in new and obscure language. Yet there was in Imagism a new idea as well as a new term, and this idea was best expressed in the beginning by Hulme. It was more than an idea with Hulme; it was his whole philosophy. He maintained that real communication between human beings is made only by means of images. His belief was that "Thought is prior to language and consists in the simultaneous presentation to the mind of two different images."[12] These images form a "visual chord" in the mind—a mental image which unites them. In order to communicate thought, there must then be what he called the "passage from the Eye to the Voice," or the process of forming sounds which stand for images. All language, according to Hulme's view, originates in word-images, and in all real communication, "Each *word* must be an image *seen*, not a counter." But by natural decay, words lose their significance as images, and so cease to communicate—unless revived by fresh associations and unexpected combinations. In the poetic use of words, language is restored to communicative power, by being infused with new images. Poetry differs from ordinary speech and from prose in the respect that "It always endeavors to arrest you, and to make you continuously see a physical thing, to prevent you gliding through an abstract process. It chooses fresh epithets and fresh metaphors, not so much because they are new, and we are tired of the old, but because the old cease to convey a physical thing and become abstract counters."[13] It is the visual content of language, then, which makes it communicative, and it is the visual accuracy of poetry which makes it more communicative than prose—"It is not a counter language, but a visual concrete

[12] Hulme, "Notes on Language and Style," *Further Speculations*, 84.
[13] Hulme, "Romanticism and Classicism," *Speculations*, 134-35.

contra romantics.

one," Hulme said. He meant, of course, that at its best poetry was visual and concrete, not that all of what passed for poetry was really of this kind. He was convinced, indeed, that most of the poetry written at the turn of the century was abstract and uncommunicative; it had ceased making new images, and was simply repeating old ones in pretty patterns of sound, "I think that there is an increasing proportion of people who simply can't stand Swinburne," was his blunt way of putting it. He argued that "a period of exhaustion seems to me to have been reached in romanticism," and predicted a new "classical" tendency in poetry in which it would become "dry" and "hard," meaning that it would become visual, concrete, and communicative once again. The poet, in Hulme's view, "must continually be creating new images, and his sincerity may be measured by the number of his images," for his principle was that "Images in verse are not mere decoration, but the very essence of an intuitive language."

Hulme's view of the poetic image became a basic assumption of the New Criticism—the assumption that poetic language is metaphorical rather than logical—that is, that the so-called "figures of speech" which poetry uses are really a more effective way of communicating meaning than either "plain talk" or the most lucid logical exposition. However, at the time he made it, Hulme's view of the poetic image was an authentic new insight into the poetic process, and it paved the way for the experiments in poetic technique which the Imagists undertook and which later poets carried forward. As Pound said in one of his definitions of the new movement, "The point of Imagisme is that it does not use images as ornaments. The image is itself the speech."[14] Both Hulme and Pound were consistent in maintaining that the principle was not new, that the intrinsic value of the image was to be seen in the best poetry of all languages and all times. Pound, for example, praised Dante primarily for the vividness of his images, and held that "Dante's 'Paradiso' is the most wonderful image." Their concentration on the image, and their search among the traditions of world poetry for fresh uses of imagery, in time resulted in a new kind of English poetry—a poetry in which the image was not a means but an end: the image was not a part of the poem; it *was* the poem.

What is the image of the Imagist poem? Essentially, it is a

[14] Pound, "Vorticism," *Fortnightly Review, XCVI,* n.s. (Sept. 1, 1914), 469.

moment of revealed truth, rather than a structure of consecutive events or thoughts. The plot or argument of older poetry is replaced by a single, dominant image, or a quick succession of related images: its effect is meant to be instantaneous rather than cumulative. And most often, the image is drawn from common life—either natural, as in H.D.'s sea or Sandburg's fog, or man-made, as in Williams' red wheelbarrow or Pound's subway station; but it may sometimes be drawn from objects or actions of the remote past, as in H.D.'s "Epigram," or Aldington's "Lesbia." Whatever its source, the test of the image was that it be rendered exactly, in as few words as possible and with the maximum of visual content. Imagist poetry aimed at complete objectivity, leaving out all rational and moral comment, for behind it was the belief that only the image communicates meaning. The sparer, starker, more striking the image, the better the poem.

This is not to say, however, that the images were to be created in a vacuum, free of all human significance. No true poem can be without human content; but in the Imagist poem, the human content is implied rather than stated. It is implied in the very choice of the image, as well as in the tone with which the image is treated. Even the shortest Imagist poems are a "criticism of life," to apply Matthew Arnold's test for poetry: Williams' red wheelbarrow, that most useful and simple of man-made implements, upon which "so much depends," is as human and real a thing, as necessary a part of our experience, as Sandburg's fog, with its mysterious, catlike movement into our senses and out again, or as the sea, cool, dark, and green as a grove of pines, in H.D.'s "Oread." Pound's "L'Art, 1910," on the other hand, is clearly meant to be a satirical commentary on its subject, while Eliot's "Preludes" imply the strongest moral criticism of the images of the modern city which they evoke. Imagist poems differ from other poems in leaving more to the reader to interpret, not in containing less of human significance. They are in this respect like the Japanese haiku, which was one of their models, though they differ from the haiku in being less restrictive in subject (classical haikus were almost exclusively nature images) and in length (Japanese haikus were traditionally seventeen syllables long). Imagist poems, like the haiku, were meant to be read and re-read, to be meditated upon, until the full significance of the image had communicated itself.

How much meaning may be concentrated in a single Imagist poem is well illustrated by the account which Pound once gave of the writing of his "In a Station of the Metro," one of the briefest and most celebrated of Imagist poems. This account amounts to a practicing definition of the Imagist poem; it is also a description fascinating in itself of the inner process by which a poem of this type might be composed:

Three years ago in Paris I got out of a "metro" train at La Concorde, and saw suddenly a beautiful face, and then another and another, and then a beautiful child's face, and then another beautiful woman, and I tried all that day to find words for what this had meant to me, and I could not find any words that seemed to me worthy, or as lovely as that sudden emotion. And that evening, as I went home along the Rue Raynouard, I was still trying, and I found, suddenly, the expression. I do not mean that I found words, but there came an equation . . . not in speech, but in little splotches of color. It was just that—a "pattern," or hardly a pattern, if by "pattern" you mean something with a "repeat" in it. But it was a word, the beginning, for me, of a language in color. . .

A Chinaman said long ago that if a man can't say what he has to say in twelve lines he had better keep quiet. The Japanese have evolved the still shorter form of the *hokku*.

The fallen blossom flies back to its branch:
A butterfly.

That is the substance of a well-known *hokku*....

The "one-image poem" is a form of super-position, that is to say it is one idea set on top of another. I found it useful in getting out of the impasse in which I had been left by my metro emotion. I wrote a thirty-line poem, and destroyed it because it was what we call work "of second intensity." Six months later I made a poem half that length; a year later I made the following *hokku*-like sentence:

The apparition of these faces in the crowd;
Petals on a wet, black bough.

I dare say it is meaningless unless one has drifted into a certain vein of thought. In a poem of this sort one is trying to record the precise instant when a thing outward and objective transforms itself, or darts into a thing inward and subjective.[15]

---

[15] Pound, "Vorticism," *Fortnightly Review*, 465–67.

There is in this account the working out of all the Imagist principles—beginning with a sudden striking visual image, then the forming of a "visual chord" or pattern of colors in the mind, then the search for the exact words to express it, the deliberate effort at concentration, and finally the use of a foreign poetic model to produce the crystallization that becomes the finished poem. It is as instructive an example as one could wish of the condensation which the Imagist discipline sought to achieve.

The example also proves that the Imagist poem was not a mere imitation, or translation, of a work in another language. Neither the subject nor the form of Pound's poem is in any way exotic, but comes directly from the experience of an urbane and widely traveled modern consciousness. Though there were many foreign influences upon the Imagist poem, none of them kept it from becoming a distinctly English form, capable of reproducing itself independently of its widely scattered sources. This adaptability is true not only of the comparatively remote Oriental and classical influences, but also of that which was nearest in time and place: the French Symbolist influence. But since this influence affected Imagist poetry more directly than any other, a final word ought to be said about the difference between the Imagist poem and the Symbolist poem—the difference, that is, between Imagism and Symbolism as modes of poetic communication.

3. The Image and the Symbol

It is generally agreed that all modern European poetry, including the English and American varieties, has its origin in the school of French poets which began with Baudelaire and continued through Verlaine, Rimbaud, Mallarmé, Corbière, Laforgue, and Valéry. The direct influence of one or more of these poets on many of the major English and American poets of the twentieth century can readily be traced. Moreover, there is the clear fact that during the decade of Imagist experiments the work of contemporary French poets was discussed more than those of any other nationality—article after article on modern French poetry was written by Pound, by Aldington, by Flint, by Amy Lowell, and published in the same magazines in which Imagist poetry was appearing.

All of these cross-channel currents have been carefully studied in René Taupin's book on the influence of French Symbolism on American poetry of the Imagist period. In it, Taupin compared the effects of Symbolist poems with those of Imagist poems, and concluded, somewhat surprisingly, that "free verse" and vers libre are not synonymous, since the French language tends to give equal weight to each spoken syllable, while in the English language syllables vary greatly in quantity according to whether they are stressed or unstressed. In this respect, "free verse" may be said to be more natural to English than to French, since regularity of rhythm is less a property of the English language than of the French—all English verse must be in some sense "free," however strict the metrical pattern. Thus, if "free verse" was French in origin, it became English by natural adaptation. Taupin also pointed out the different use of poetic imagery in Imagism and in Symbolism. The Symbolists used images as part of a poem; the Imagists thought of an image as a complete poem. The Symbolists tried for diffuseness and suggestiveness; the Imagists insisted on concentration and directness. Taupin said of the Imagists, "The pleasure of their poetry is not the satisfaction of discovering little by little, but of seizing at a single blow, in the fullest vitality, the image, a fusion of reality in words."[16] But it was Taupin's conclusion, that however great the divergence of technique and language, "between the 'image' of the Imagists and the 'symbol' of the Symbolists there is a difference only of precision."[17]

This is the crucial distinction, for Imagism was chiefly a movement toward making the poetic figure—be it simple metaphor or complex symbol—more definite and more real. The Imagist experiments were based on the belief, expressed in Pound's "A Few Don'ts of an Imagiste" in 1913, that "the natural object is always the adequate symbol." Pound had expressed this view more fully the year before, in his "Credo" under the heading of "Symbols":

I believe that the proper and perfect symbol is the natural object, that if a man use "symbols" he must so use them that their symbolic function does not obtrude; so that a sense, and the poetic quality of the passage, is not lost to those who do not understand the symbol

---

[16] Taupin, 96.
[17] Taupin, 93.

as such, to whom, for instance, a hawk is a hawk.[18]

Pound seems to have made the same distinction between the image and the symbol, then, that is usually made between symbolism and allegory: that the symbolic meaning must have its source in the literal meaning, and not be imposed upon it. He seems to have regarded French Symbolism as tending toward the allegorical, and wanted Imagism to be directed toward the realistic. Believing that Symbolism suffered from too much vagueness, he was willing to let Imagism suffer, if it must, from too much concreteness: to be purely descriptive was better than to be purely "symbolic."

All symbolism was not ruled out of the Imagist poem, however. It should be remembered that Pound subscribed to a belief in "absolute rhythm," and in an essay of 1914 he admitted to "a like belief in a sort of permanent metaphor," which, as he said,—"is, as I understand it, 'symbolism' in its profounder sense."[19] He recognized that to believe in "absolute rhythm" and "permanent metaphor" was tantamount to believing in "a permanent world"— an ideal world, in other words, beyond or within the world of appearances, which is the basis for all true symbolism. Since the Imagist poem aimed at being an exact equivalent in rhythm and image for the poet's experience, it may properly be viewed as an advanced stage of the tradition that began with Baudelaire's famous sonnet on the "Correspondances"—the touchstone of French Symbolism—and that later received critical expression in Eliot's idea of the "objective correlative": a tradition in which every effort at realism was also an effort at symbolism, since in a poem no object ever exists for itself alone, but is an "intellectual and emotional complex" as well.

If "Imagisme is not symbolism," as Pound insisted, it is a direct descendant: given the different native traditions and the different historical moments, the "Image" and the "Symbol" are at their best aesthetic equivalents, the difference being, as Taupin admirably stated it, "a difference only of precision."

---

[18] This quotation, first published in *Poetry and Drama* in 1912, is included in "A Retrospect," a collection of Pound's various writings on Imagism, published in *Pavannes and Divisions* (1918), and later in *The Literary Essays of Ezra Pound,* ed. T.S. Eliot (New York: New Directions, 1954), 3–14.

[19] Pound, "Vorticism," *Fortnightly Review,* 3.

PART IV. THE PERMANENCE OF THE IMAGIST POEM

There is no need to argue for the historical importance of Imagist poetry. It was the beginning of what we now call "modern poetry" in English. It represented the first serious effort at reforming the diction of English poetry since Wordsworth and Coleridge, and it began as a reaction to the Romantic movement, just as the Romantics had begun by reacting against their predecessors, the Neo-Classical poets. But it went beyond simple reform and reaction to make the first concerted attempt since Elizabethan times at establishing a new English cadence, a "free verse" based on natural speech rhythm, to replace the blank verse, or iambic pentameter, line that had been the standard in English poetry since the Elizabethan period. It also experimented with the poetic symbol, striving to make it more visual, concrete, and concentrated in its effect, maintaining that "the natural object is always the adequate symbol," and that it should be presented without explicit moral interpretation, since the image itself was the means of verbal expression. All these efforts reached their fulfillment in the major achievements of modern English poetry.

But no poetic movement, however important historically, is better than the poems it produces. Pound said in 1916, after he had parted company with the Imagists, that "Perhaps a few good poems have come from the new method, and if so it is justified."[20]

The full justification was slow to come, however, for few serious critics paid Imagist poetry more than passing notice for more than half a century after it became literary history.[21] Even Eliot, in calling it "the starting-point of modern poetry," added that it was "a

---

[20] Pound, "A Retrospect," *Literary Essays of Ezra Pound*, 3.

[21] Still largely true of American critics, in spite of two full-sized books on the Imagist movement: Glenn Hughes' *Imagism and the Imagists*, published by Stanford University Press in 1931, and Stanley Coffman's *Imagism: A Chapter for the History of Modern Poetry*, published by the University of Oklahoma Press in 1951. British critics, however, have paid more serious attention to Imagism, with some, like Frank Kermode, in *Romantic Image* (London: Routledge & Kegan Paul, 1957) and Graham Hough, in *Reflections on a Literary Revolution* (Washington: Catholic University Press, 1960) using it as a means of disparaging modern poetry. But others, especially Herbert Read in *The Tenth Muse*, and even more, Stephen Spender in *The Struggle of the Modern* (Berkeley: U. of California Press, 1963) have seen it as essential to the development of modern poetic style. Whatever their point of view, both American and British critics have acknowledged the fundamental importance of Imagism to modern poetry in English.

movement which on the whole, is chiefly important because of the stimulus it gave to later developments." Perhaps Pound may be partly blamed for the neglect into which Imagism fell, because of the jealous attacks he made on the movement after he left it, and his swift adoption of a new and even shorter-lived movement called "Vorticism." But it seems more probable that Imagist poetry lacked a comprehensive collection before 1963, when this anthology first appeared, affirming Imagism's historical importance and identifying those poems that best represented it.

Thus the value of this first complete anthology of Imagist poems (the very first, *Des Imagistes*, which Pound edited in 1914, had to be partial, since the movement was just getting under way) is that it brought together not only the best of the poems which appeared in the four original anthologies, but also the best of all the poems which were published during the Imagist period, whether in *Poetry*, the *Egoist*, the *Little Review*, or more out-of-the-way places—all the poems, that is to say, which might reasonably be associated with the Imagist experiments, and which contributed to the development of a distinctive modern poetic form.

That a number of well-known anthology pieces can legitimately be called "Imagist" should help to counteract the frequent charge— which F. 0. Matthiessen, for instance, voiced in the introduction to his *Oxford Book of American Verse* that the movement created "very few lasting works." As for the more serious charge, which Randall Jarrell made in his introduction to the *Selected Poems of William Carlos Williams*—namely, that Williams, Marianne Moore, and Wallace Stevens "did their first good work in an odd climate of poetic opinion," where the "expectations of behavior were Imagist," the "metrical demands were minimal," and the "ideals of organization were mosaic"—it can only be said that without the influence of Imagism their poetry would be very different, and probably not nearly so original nor so excellent. Because their first distinctive work was written during the Imagist period, it is best understood in the context of other Imagist poems, not apart from them.

It is true that both Williams and Stevens recognized the limits of Imagism, and went considerably beyond it in their later poetry. Williams felt, as was noted earlier, that "Imagism failed because it lost structural necessity," while Stevens once observed: "Not all objects are equal. The vice of imagism was that it did not recognize this."[22] Yet Stevens showed in another note that he understood well the purpose of Imagism: "The bare image and the image as a symbol are the contrast: the image without meaning and the image as meaning." Furthermore, Stevens said of Williams that "Imagism (as one of Williams's many involvements, however long ago) is not something superficial. It obeys an instinct. Moreover, Imagism is an ancient phase of poetry. It is something permanent."[23] And Williams himself wrote a letter to Pound in 1932, in which he declared: "Returning to the writing of verse, which is the only thing that concerns us after all: certainly there is nothing for it but to go on with a complex quantitative music and to further accuracy of image..."[24] For these poets, then, Imagism might have failed as a movement, but as a theory it succeeded, and in the later poems of both Williams and Stevens there is convincing proof that the Imagist discipline continued to work on them to the end of their lives.

A more pertinent criticism was that of R. P. Blackmur, who once described Williams' poetry as "the Imagism of 1912 self-transcended."[25] The remark is just enough to be extended to each of the important poets who contributed to the Imagist movement, for they are all "Imagists of 1912 self-transcended." There have really been few other kinds of poets in the twentieth century, so far-reaching has the influence of Imagism been. Though short-lived as a movement, its principles were carried forward in the mature poetry of nearly every one of the major Modernist poets.

In Williams' letter to Pound is the clue to what the full importance of Imagist poetry must be. For in saying that "there is nothing for it but to go on with a complex quantitative music and to further accuracy of the image," Williams was pointing to the fact that most of the later experiments in modern English poetry were really extensions of the original Imagist program. Indeed, after all, what are the longer poems of Williams, Pound, or Eliot but aggregate Imagist poems, set in a sort of mosaic pattern around a dominant image—a super-image, like *The Waste Land*, for example,

---

[22] Stevens, "Adagia," in *Opus Posthumous,* ed. Samuel F. Morse (New York: Alfred Knopf, 1957), 161.

[23] Stevens, "Rubbings of Reality," *Opus Posthumous*, 258.

[24] Williams, *Selected Letters* (New York: McDowell, Obolensky, 1957), 126.

25 Blackmur, "Lord Tennyson's Scissors: 1912–50," in *Form and Value in M(Poetry* (New York: Doubleday Anchor Books, 1957), 374.

or arranged in successive "ideograms," as in the *Cantos*? And in even the longest of them, in Williams' *Paterson*, Pound's *Cantos*, or Eliot's *Four Quartets*, the effect of instantaneous perception, or simultaneity, is as notable as in the shortest Imagist poem: "all time is eternally present," as Eliot says at the opening of the *Four Quartets*, and past, present, and future are fused in those moments of incarnation which form the principal subject of the poem.

If Imagist poetry itself is minor poetry, therefore, it has had its apotheosis in the major Modernist long poems of the twentieth century—-some of which, like Hart Crane's *The Bridge*, for example, were written outside the sphere of Imagist activity, but not of Imagist influence. In the development of modern English and American poetry, there has been, as Herbert Read said in a late essay, "one clear line of progress—the isolation and clarification of the image, and the perfecting of a diction that would leave the image unclouded by rhetoric or sentiment."[26]

The permanent value of Imagist poetry is no greater, and certainly it is no less, than that of modern poetry in general. If the mature poems of Pound and Eliot, Lawrence and Stevens, Williams and Marianne Moore-—not to speak of others-—prove valuable beyond the age in which they were written, then Imagist poetry, which is basic to their work, must be valuable, too. "Preludes," Eliot's title, seems a proper way of describing all Imagist poems, for they were the prelude to the full orchestration of the modern poem. And it seems safe to say that, should any new metamorphoses of the modern poetic tradition occur, new Imagist poems will be written. For whenever precision and clarity of language combine with natural musical form, new Imagist poems are being created, whatever names may be given them.

WILLIAM PRATT
Oxford, Ohio

[26] Read, "The Image in Modern English Poetry," in *The Tenth Muse*, 137.

The Imagist Poem

AUTUMN

A touch of cold in the Autumn night
I walked abroad,
And saw the ruddy moon lean over a hedge
Like a red-faced farmer.
I did not stop to speak, but nodded;
And round about were the wistful stars
With white faces like town children

CONVERSION

Light-hearted I walked into the valley wood
In the time of hyacinths,
Till beauty like a scented cloth
Cast over, stifled me, I was bound
Motionless and faint of breath
By loveliness that is her own eunuch.
Now pass I to the final river
Ignominiously, in a sack, without sound,
As any peeping Turk to the Bosphorus.

FRAGMENTS

I

With a courtly bow the bent tree sighed
May I present you to my friend the sun.

II

Three birds flew over the red wall into the pit of the setting sun.
O daring, doomed birds that pass from my sight.

III

I walked into the wood in June
And suddenly Beauty, like a thick scented veil,
Stifled me,
Tripped me up, tight round my limbs,
Arrested me.

ABOVE THE DOCK

Above the quiet dock in midnight,
Tangled in the tall mast's corded height,
Hangs the moon. What seemed so far away
Is but a child's balloon, forgotten after play.

THE MAN IN THE CROW'S NEST

Strange to me sounds the wind that blows
By the masthead in the lonely night.
Maybe 'tis the sea whistling—feigning joy
To hide its fright
Like a village boy
That, trembling, past the churchyard goes.

THE POET

Over a large table, smooth, he leaned in ecstasies,
In a dream.
He had been to woods, and talked and walked with trees.
Had left the world
And brought back round globes and stone images,
Of gems, colors, hard and definite.
With these he played, in a dream,
On the smooth table.

MANA ABODA[1]

*Beauty is the marking-time, the stationary vibration, the feigned
ecstasy of any arrested impulse unable to reach its natural end.*

Mana Aboda, whose bent form
The sky in arched circle is,
Seems ever for an unknown grief to mourn.
Yet on a day I heard her cry:
"I weary of the roses and the singing poets—
Josephs all, not tall enough to try."

THE EMBANKMENT

(The fantasia of a fallen gentleman on a cold, bitter night)

Once, in finesse of fiddles found I ecstasy,
In a flash of gold heels on the hard pavement.
Now see I
That warmth's the very stuff of poesy.
Oh, God, make small
The old star-eaten blanket of the sky,
That I may fold it round me and in comfort lie.

---

[1] Polynesian deity, the elemental force of nature embodied in a person or thing.

CHRYSANTHEMUMS

O golden-red and tall chrysanthemums,
you are the graceful soul of the china vase
wherein you stand
amid your leaves.

O quiet room,
you are the symbol of my patient heart.
O flowers of flame, O tall chrysanthemums,
my love who comes

will wave wide ripples of disquiet there,
and a great tide of the eternal sea
will rise at her approach,
and surge to song.

O quiet room, O flame chrysanthemums,
images of my heart and its proud love,
you have no presage of the power that comes
to fill with anguish the essential calm.

O calm wrought face, O sphinx behind the door,
her hand is on the latch.

BEGGAR

In the gutter
piping his sadness
an old man stands,
bent and shriveled,
beard draggled,
eyes dead.

Huddled and mean,
shivering in threadbare clothes—
winds beat him,
hunger bites him,
forlorn, a whistle in his hands,
piping.

Hark! The strange quality
Of his sorrowful music,
wind from an empty belly
wrought magically
into the wind,—

pattern of silver on bronze.

FRAGMENT

. . . That night I loved you
in the candlelight.
Your golden hair
strewed the sweet whiteness of the pillows
and the counterpane.
0 the darkness of the corners,
the warm air, and the stars
framed in the casement of the ships' lights!
The waves lapped into the harbor;
the boats creaked;
a man's voice sang out on the quay;
and you loved me.
In your love were the tall tree fuchsias,
the blue of the hortensias, the scarlet nasturtiums,
the trees on the hills,
the roads we had covered,
and the sea that had borne your body
before the rocks of Hartland.
You loved me with these
and with the kindness of people,
country folk, sailors and fishermen,
and the old lady who had lodged us and supped us.
You loved me with yourself
that was these and more,
changed as the earth is changed
into the bloom of flowers.

THE SWAN

Under the lily shadow
and the gold
and the blue and mauve
that the whin and the lilac
pour down on the water,
the fishes quiver.

Over the green cold leaves
and the rippled silver
and the tarnished copper
of its neck and beak,
toward the deep black water
beneath the arches,
the swan floats slowly.

Into the dark of the arch the swan floats
and into the black depth of my sorrow
it bears a white rose of flame.

THE TREE

I stood still and was a tree amid the wood,
Knowing the truth of things unseen before;
Of Daphne and the laurel bow
And that god-fearing couple old
That grew elm-oak amid the wold.
'Twas not until the gods had been
Kindly entreated, and been brought within
Unto the hearth of their heart's home
That they might do this wonder thing;
Nathless I have been a tree amid the wood
And many a new thing understood
That was rank folly to my head before.

IN A STATION OF THE METRO

The apparition of these faces in the crowd;
Petals on a wet, black bough.

L'ART, 1910

Green arsenic smeared on an egg-white cloth,
Crushed strawberries! Come, let us feast our eyes.

ALBA

As cool as the pale wet leaves
                              of lily-of-the-valley
She lay beside me in the dawn.

GENTILDONNA

She passed and left no quiver in the veins, who
                now
Moving among the trees, and clinging
                        in the air she severed,
Fanning the grass she walked on then, endures:

Grey olive leaves beneath a rain-cold sky.

APRIL

Three spirits came to me
And drew me apart
To where the olive boughs
Lay stripped upon the ground:
Pale carnage beneath bright mist.

HEATHER

The black panther treads at my side,
And above my fingers
There float the petal-like flames.

The milk-white girls
Unbend from the holly-trees,
And their snow-white leopard
Watches to follow our trace.

THE RETURN

See, they return; ah, see the tentative
Movements, and the slow feet,
The trouble in the pace and the uncertain
Wavering!
See, they return, one, and by one,
With fear, as half-awakened;
As if the snow should hesitate
And murmur in the wind,
        and half turn back;
These were the "Wing'd-with-Awe,"
        Inviolable.

Gods of the winged shoe!
With them the silver hounds,
        sniffing the trace of air!

Haie! Haie!
        These were the swift to harry;
These the keen-scented;
These were the souls of blood.
Slow on the leash,
pallid the leash-men!

DORIA
Δώρια [1]

Be in me as the eternal moods
              of the bleak wind, and not
As transient things are
        gaiety of flowers.
Have me in the strong loneliness
        of sunless cliffs
And of grey waters.
        Let the gods speak softly of us
In days hereafter,
        The shadowy flowers of Orcus[2]
    Remember thee.

IMERRO
ἱμέρρω [3]

Thy soul
Grown delicate with satieties,
Atthis.
O Atthis,
I long for thy lips.
I long for thy narrow breasts,
Thou restless, ungathered.

[1] Greek for "Dorian girl."
[2] Another name for the Underworld.
[3] A Greek word meaning "I long for you."

THE SPRING
'Ηρι μεν άί τε κυδώνιαι
            —Ibycus[1]

Cydonian Spring with her attendant train,
Maelids and water-girls,
Stepping beneath a boisterous wind from
Thrace,
Throughout this sylvan place
Spreads the bright tips,
And every vine-stock is
Clad in new brilliancies.
                    And wild desire
Falls like black lightning.
0 bewildered heart,
Though every branch have back what last year lost,
She, who moved here amid the cyclamen,
Moves only now a clinging tenuous ghost.

---

[1] "In springtime the Kydonian quinces..."—The opening line of a Greek lyric by
Ibycus on which this poem is based.

THE COMING OF WAR: ACTAEON

An image of Lethe,
          and the fields
Full of faint light
          but golden,
Gray cliffs,
          and beneath them
A sea
Harsher than granite,
          unstill, never ceasing;
High forms
          with the movement of gods,
Perilous aspect;
          And one said:
"This is Actaeon."
          Actaeon of golden greaves!
Over fair meadows,
Over the cool face of that field,
Unstill, ever moving
Hosts of an ancient people,
The silent cortège.

THE JEWEL STAIRS' GRIEVANCE

The jewelled steps are already quite white with dew,
it is so late that the dew soaks my gauze stockings,
And I let down the crystal curtain
And watch the moon through the clear autumn.

NOTE: *Jewel stairs, therefore a palace. Grievance, therefore there is something to
complain of. Gauze stockings, therefore a court lady, not a servant who complains. Clear
autumn, therefore he has no excuse on account of weather. Also she has come early, for
the dew has not merely whitened the stairs, but has soaked her stockings. The poem is
especially prized because she utters no direct reproach.*

TS'AI CHI'H[1]

The petals fall in the fountain,
      The orange-colored rose-leaves,
Their ochre clings to the stone.

FAN-PIECE, FOR HER IMPERIAL LORD

O fan of white silk,
      clear as frost on the grass-blade,
You also are laid aside.

[1] The name of an ancient Chinese poet whose work Pound liberally translated and
condensed. For a full discussion of Pound's use of Chinese sources, see Zhaoming
Qian, *Orientalism and Modernism: The Legacy of China in Pound and Williams*
(Durham & London: Duke University Press, 1995), 39–47.

LIU CH'E[1]

The rustling of the silk is discontinued,
Dust drifts over the court-yard,
There is no sound of foot-fall, and the leaves
Scurry into heaps and lie still,
And she the rejoicer of the heart is beneath them:

A wet leaf that clings to the threshold.

SEPARATION ON THE RIVER KIANG

Ko-Jin goes west from Ko-kaku-ro,
The smoke-flowers are blurred over the river.
His lone sail blots the far sky.
And now I see only the river,
        The long Kiang, reaching heaven.

[1] *Ibid.*

THE RIVER-MERCHANT'S WIFE: A LETTER

While my hair was still cut straight across my forehead
I walked about the front gate, pulling flowers.
You came by on bamboo stilts, playing horse,
You walked about my seat, playing with blue plums.
And we went on living in the village of Chokan:
Two small people, without dislike or suspicion.

At fourteen, I married My Lord you.
I never laughed, being bashful.
Lowering my head, I looked at the wall.
Called to, a thousand times, I never looked back.

At fifteen I stopped scowling,
I desired my dust to be mingled with yours
Forever and forever and forever.
Why should I climb the lookout?

At sixteen, you departed.
You went into far Ku-to-yen, by the river of swirling eddies,
And you have been gone five months.
The monkeys make sorrowful noise overhead.
You dragged your feet when you went out.
By the gate now, the moss is grown, the different mosses,
Too deep to clear them away!
The leaves fall early this autumn, in wind.
The paired butterflies are already yellow with August,
Over the grass in the West garden;
They hurt me. I grow older.
If you are coming down through the narrows of the river Kiang,
Please let me know beforehand,
And I will come out to meet you
As far as Cho-fu-sa.

[Pound's Note, "After Rihaku," uses the Japanese transcription of the name of Li Po or Li Bai, celebrated Chinese poet of the Tang Dynasty]

I HEAR AN ARMY

I hear an army charging upon the land,
    And the thunder of horses plunging, foam about their knees:
Arrogant, in black armor, behind them stand,
    Disdaining the reins, with fluttering whips, the charioteers.

They cry unto the night their battle-name:
    I moan in sleep when I hear afar their whirling laughter.
They cleave the gloom of dreams, a blinding flame,
    Clanging, clanging upon the heart as upon an anvil.

They come shaking in triumph their long, green hair:
    They come out of the sea and run shouting by the shore.
My heart, have you no wisdom thus to despair?
    My love, my love, my love, why have you left me alone?

OREAD

Whirl up, sea—
whirl your pointed pines,
splash your great pines
on our rocks,
hurl your green over us,
cover us with your pools of fir.

EPIGRAM
(After the Greek)

The golden one is gone from the banquets;
She, beloved of Atimetus,
The swallow, the bright Homonoea:
Gone the dear chatterer.

THE POOL

Are you alive?
I touch you.
You quiver like a sea-fish.
I cover you with my net.
What are you—banded one?

NEVER MORE WILL THE WIND

Never more will the wind
cherish you again
never more will the rain.

Never more
shall we find you bright
in the snow and wind.

The snow is melted,
the snow is gone,
and you are flown:

Like a bird out of our hand
like a light out of our heart,
you are gone.

ORCHARD

I saw the first pear
as it fell—
the
honey-seeking, golden-banded,
the yellow swarm
was not more fleet than I,
(spare us from loveliness)
and I fell prostrate,
crying:
you have flayed us
with your blossoms,
spare us the beauty
of fruit-trees.
The honey-seeking
Paused not,
the air thundered their song,
and I alone was prostrate.

O rough-hewn
god of the orchard,
I bring an offering—
do you, alone unbeautiful,
son of the god,
spare us from loveliness:
these fallen hazel-nuts,
stripped late of their green sheaths,
grapes, red-purple,
their berries
dripping with wine,
pomegranates already broken,
and shrunken figs
and quinces untouched,
I bring you as offering.

HERMES OF THE WAYS

I

The hard sand breaks,
And the grains of it
Are clear as wine.

Far off over the leagues of it,
The wind,
Playing on the wide shore,
Piles little ridges,
And the great waves
Break over it.

But more than the many-foamed ways
Of the sea,
I know him
Of the triple path-ways,
Hermes,
Who awaiteth.

Dubious,
Facing three ways,
Welcoming wayfarers,
He whom the sea-orchard
Shelters from the west,
From the east
Weathers sea-wind;
Fronts the great dunes.

Wind rushes
Over the dunes,
And the coarse, salt-crusted grass
Answers.
Heu,
it whips round my ankles!

II

Small is
This white stream,
Flowing below ground
From the poplar-shaded hill,
But the water is sweet.

Apples on the small trees
Are hard,
Too small,
Too late ripened
By a desperate sun
That struggles through sea-mist.

The boughs of the trees
Are twisted
By many bafflings;
Twisted are
The small-leafed boughs.
But the shadow of them
Is not the shadow of the mast head
Nor of the torn sails.

Hermes, Hermes,
The great sea foamed,
Gnashed its teeth about me;
But you have waited,
Where sea-grass tangles with
Shore-grass.

HEAT

O wind, rend open the heat,
cut apart the heat,
rend it to tatters.

Fruit cannot drop
through this thick air—
fruit cannot fall into heat
that presses up and blunts
the points of pears
and rounds the grapes.

Cut the heat—
plough through it,
turning it on either side
of your path.

PEAR TREE

Silver dust,
lifted from the earth,
higher than my arms reach,
you have mounted,
O, silver,
higher than my arms reach,
you front us with great mass;

no flower ever opened
so staunch a white leaf,
no flower ever parted silver
from such rare silver;

O, white pear,
your flower-tufts
thick on the branch
bring summer and ripe fruits
in their purple hearts.

STORM

I

You crash over the trees,
You crack the live branch:
the branch is white,
the green crushed,
each leaf is rent like split wood.

II

You burden the trees
with black drops,
you swirl and crash:
you have broken off a weighted leaf
in the wind—
it is hurled out,
whirls up and sinks,
a green stone.

SONG

You are as gold
as the half-ripe grain
that merges to gold again,
as white as the white rain
that beats through
the half-opened flowers
of the great flower tufts
thick on the black limbs
of an Illyrian apple bough.

Can honey distill such fragrance
As your bright hair—
For your face is as fair as rain,
yet as rain that lies clear
on white honey-comb,
lends radiance to the white wax,
so your hair on your brow
casts light for a shadow.

EVENING

The light passes
from ridge to ridge,
from flower to flower—
the hypaticas, wide-spread
under the light
grow faint—
the petals reach inward,
the blue tips bend
toward the bluer heart
and the flowers are lost.

The cornel-buds are still white,
But shadows dart
from the cornel-roots—
black creeps from root to root,
each leaf
cuts another leaf on the grass,
shadow seeks shadow,
then both leaf
and leaf-shadow are lost.

SEA ROSE

Rose, harsh rose,
marred and with stint of petals,
meagre flower, thin,
sparse of leaf,

more precious
than a wet rose,
single on a stem—
you are caught in the drift.

Stunted, with small leaf,
you are flung on the sands,
you are lifted
in the crisp sand
that drives in the wind.

Can the spice-rose
drip such acrid fragrance
hardened in a leaf?

HELEN

All Greece hates
the still eyes in the white face,
the lustre as of olives
where she stands,
and the white hands.

All Greece reviles
the wan face when she smiles,
hating it deeper still
when it grows wan and white,
remembering past enchantments
and past ills.

Greece sees unmoved,
God's daughter, born of love,
the beauty of cool feet
and slenderest knees,
could love indeed the maid,
only if she were laid,
white ash amid funereal cypresses.

LOVE THAT I BEAR

Love that I bear
within my heart, O speak;
tell how beneath the serpent-spotted shell,
the cygnets wait,
how the soft owl
opens and flicks with pride,
eye-lids of great bird-eyes,
when underneath its breast,
the owlets shrink and turn.

HYMN
(For Count Zinzendorf, 1700-1760)[1]

Of unguent in a jar,
We may ensample myrrh;

So were His fragrance stored,
Sealed up, compact, secure,

In flawless alabaster,
But for the spear;

This is the wound of grace,
This is the nesting-place

Of the white dove,
This is the wound of love;

The spear opened for us
The rose of purple fire,

The rose of iciest breath,
White rose of death;

The spear opened for us
The narrow way

Into the dust,
To the eternal day.

---

1 German theologian and founder of the Moravian Brethren, a Protestant sect.

LESBIA

Use no more speech now;
Let the silence spread gold hair above us
Fold on delicate fold;
You had the ivory of my life to carve.
Use no more speech.

        . . . .

And Picus of Mirandola is dead;
And all the gods they dreamed and fabled of,
Hermes, and Thoth, and Christ, are rotten now,
Rotten and dank.

        . . . .

And through it all I see your pale Greek face;
Tenderness makes me as eager as a little child
To love you

You morsel left half cold on Caesar's plate.[1]

---

[1] Line adapted from Shakespeare's Antony and Cleopatra: "You were a morsel left
half cold on Caesar's plate."

EPIGRAMS

A GIRL

You were that clear Sicilian fluting
That pains our thought even now.
You were the notes
Of cold fantastic grief
Some few found beautiful.

NEW LOVE

She has new leaves
After her dead flowers,
Like the little almond-tree
Which the frost hurt.

OCTOBER

The beech-leaves are silver
For lack of the tree's blood.

At your kiss my lips
Become like the autumn beech-leaves.

POEM

I have drifted along this river
Until I moored my boat
By these crossed trunks.

Here the mist moves
Over fragile leaves and rushes,
Colorless waters and brown, fading hills.

You have come from beneath the trees
And move within the mist,
A floating leaf.

O blue flower of the evening,
You have touched my face
With your leaves of silver.

Love me, for I must depart.

CAPTIVE

They have torn the gold tettinx
From my hair;
And wrenched the bronze sandals
From my ankles.

They have taken from me my friend
Who knew the holy wisdom of poets,
Who had drunk at the feast
Where Simonides sang.

No more do I walk the calm gardens
In the white mist of olives;
No more do I take the rose-crown
From the white hands of a maiden.

I, who was free, am a slave;
The Muses have forgotten me,
The gods do not hear me.

Here there are no flowers to love;
But afar off I dream that I see
Bent poppies and the deathless asphodel.

AT THE BRITISH MUSEUM

I turn the page and read:
"I dream of silent verses where the rhyme
Glides noiseless as an oar."

The heavy musty air, the black desks,
The bent heads and the rustling noises
In the great dome
Vanish . . .

And
The sun hangs in the cobalt-blue sky,
The boat drifts over the lake shallows,
The fishes skim like umber shades through the undulating weeds,
The oleanders drop their rosy petals on the lawns,
And the swallows dive and swirl and whistle
About the cleft battlements of Can Grande's castle. . .[1]

[1] Place where Dante, in exile from Florence, wrote *The Divine Comedy*.

IMAGES

I

Like a gondola of green scented fruits
Drifting along the dank canals at Venice,
You, O exquisite one,
Have entered my desolate city.

II

The blue smoke leaps
Like swirling clouds of birds vanishing.
So my love leaps forth towards you,
Vanishes and is renewed.

III

A rose-yellow moon in a pale sky
When the sunset is faint vermilion
In the mist among the tree-boughs,
Art thou to me.

IV

As a young beech-tree on the edge of a forest
Stands still in the evening,
Yet shudders through all its leaves in the light air
And seems to fear the stars
So are you still and so tremble.

V

The red deer are high on the mountain,
They are beyond the last pine trees.
And my desires have run with them.

VI

The flower which the wind has shaken
Is soon filled again with rain;
So does my mind fill slowly with misgiving
Until you return.

EVENING

The chimneys, rank on rank,
Cut the clear sky;
The moon
With a rag of gauze about her loins
Poses among them, an awkward Venus—

And here am I looking wantonly at her
Over the kitchen sink.

AUX IMAGISTES

I think I have never been so exalted
As I am now by you,
O frost bitten blossoms,
That are unfolding your wings
From out the envious black branches.

Bloom quickly and make much of the sunshine
The twigs conspire against you!
Hear them!
They hold you from behind!

You shall not take wing
Except wing by wing, brokenly,
And yet—
Even they
Shall not endure for ever.

THE RED WHEELBARROW

so much depends
upon

a red wheel
barrow

glazed with rain
water

beside the white
chickens.

THE LOCUST TREE IN FLOWER

Among
of
green

stiff
old
bright

broken
branch
come

white
sweet
May
again

METRIC FIGURE

There is a bird in the poplars!
It is the sun!
The leaves are little yellow fish
swimming in the river.
The bird skims above them,
day is on his wings.
Phoebus!
It is he that is making
the great gleam among the poplars!
It is his singing
outshines the noise
of leaves clashing in the wind.

NANTUCKET

Flowers through the window
lavender and yellow

changed by white curtains—
Smell of cleanliness—

Sunshine of late afternoon—
On the glass tray

a glass pitcher, the tumbler
turned down, by which

a key is lying—And the
immaculate white bed

FLOWERS BY THE SEA

When over the flowery, sharp pasture's
edge, unseen, the salt ocean

lifts its form—chicory and daisies
tied, released, seem hardly flowers alone

but color and the movement—or the shape
perhaps—of restlessness, whereas

the sea is circled and sways
peacefully upon its plantlike stem

POEM

As the cat
climbed over
the top of

the jamcloset
first the right
forefoot

carefully then
the hind
stepped down

into the pit of
the empty
flowerpot

DAISY

The dayseye hugging the earth
In August, ha! Spring is
gone down in purple,
weeds stand high in the corn,
the rainbeaten furrow
is clotted with sorrel
and crabgrass, the
branch is black under
the heavy mass of the leaves—
The sun is upon a
slender green stem
ribbed lengthwise.
He lies on his back—
it is a woman also—
he regards his former
    majesty and
round the yellow center,
split and creviced and done into
minute flowerheads, he sends out
his twenty rays—a little
and the wind is among them
to grow cool there!

    One turns the thing over
in his hand and looks
at it from the rear: brownedged,
green and pointed scales
armor his yellow.

        But turn and turn,
the crisp petals remain
brief, translucent, greenfastened,
barely touching at the edges:
blades of limpid seashell.

QUEEN-ANN'S-LACE

Her body is not so white as
Anemone petals nor so smooth—nor
so remote a thing. It is a field
of the wild carrot taking
the field by force; the grass
does not raise above it.
Here is no question of whiteness,
white as can be, with a purple mole
at the center of each flower.
Each flower is a hand's span of
her whiteness. Wherever
his hand has lain there is
a tiny purple blemish. Each part
is a blossom under his touch
to which the fibres of her being
stem one by one, each to its end,
until the whole field is a
white desire, empty, a single stem,
a cluster, flower by flower,
a pious wish to whiteness gone over—
or nothing.

IRIS

a burst of iris so that
come down for
breakfast

we searched through the
rooms for
that

sweetest odor and at
first could not
find its

source then a blue as
of the sea
struck

startling us from among
those trumpeting
petals

DAWN

Ecstatic bird songs pound
the hollow vastness of the sky
with metallic clinkings—
beating color up into it
at a far edge,—beating it, beating it
with rising, triumphant ardor,—
stirring it into warmth,
quickening in it a spreading change,—
bursting wildly against it as
dividing the horizon, a heavy sun
lifts himself—is lifted—
bit by bit above the edge
of things,—runs free at last
out into the open-! lumbering
glorified in full release upward—
       songs cease.

TO WAKEN AN OLD LADY

   Old age is
a flight of small
cheeping birds
skimming
bare trees
above a snow glaze.
Gaining and failing
they are buffeted
by a dark wind—
But what?
On harsh weedstalks
the flock has rested,
the snow
is covered with broken
seedhusks
and the wind tempered
by a shrill
piping of plenty.

PORTRAIT OF A LADY

Your thighs are appletrees
whose blossoms touch the sky.
Which sky? The sky
where Watteau hung a lady's
slipper. Your knees
are a southern breeze—or
a gust of snow. Agh! What
sort of man was Fragonard?
—as if that answered
anything. Ah, yes—below
the knees, since the tune
drops that way, it is
one of those white summer days,
the tall grass of your ankles
flickers upon the shore—
Which shore?—
the sand clings to my lips—
Which shore?
Agh, petals maybe. How
should I know?
Which shore? Which shore?
I said petals from an appletree.

THE BULL

It is in captivity—
ringed, haltered, chained
to a drag
the bull is godlike

Unlike the cows
he lives alone, nozzles
the sweet grass gingerly
to pass the time away

He kneels, lies down
and stretching out
a foreleg licks himself
about the hoof

then stays
with half-closed eyes,
Olympian commentary on
the bright passage of days.
—The round sun
smooth his lacquer
through
the glossy pinetrees

his substance hard
as ivory or glass
through which the wind
yet plays—
              milkless

he nods
the hair between his horns
and eyes matted
with hyacinthine curls

EL HOMBRE

It's a strange courage
you give me, ancient star:

Shine alone in the sunrise
toward which you lend no part!

A SORT OF A SONG

Let the snake wait under
his weed
and the writing
be of words, slow and quick, sharp
to strike, quiet to wait,
sleepless.

—through metaphor to reconcile
the people and the stones.
Compose. (No ideas
but in things) Invent!
Saxifrage is my flower that splits
the rocks.

BIRD

Bird with outstretched
wings poised
in violate unreaching

and yet reaching
your image this November
planes

to a stop
miraculously fixed in my
arresting eyes

LANDSCAPE WITH THE FALL OF ICARUS

According to Breughel
when Icarus fell
it was spring

a farmer was ploughing
his field
the whole pageantry

of the year was
awake tingling
near

the edge of the sea
concerned
with itself

sweating in the sun
that melted
the wings' wax

unsignificantly
off the coast
there was

a splash quite unnoticed
this was
Icarus drowning.

PRELUDES

I

The winter evening settles down
With smell of steaks in passageways.
Six o'clock.
The burnt-out ends of smoky days.
And now a gusty shower wraps
The grimy scraps
Of withered leaves about your feet
And newspapers from vacant lots;
The showers beat
On broken blinds and chimney-pots,
And at the corner of the street
A lonely cab-horse steams and stamps.
And then the lighting of the lamps.

II

The morning comes to consciousness
Of faint stale smells of beer
From the sawdust-trampled street
With all its muddy feet that press
To early coffee-stands.
With the other masquerades
That time resumes,
One thinks of all the hands
That are raising dingy shades
In a thousand furnished rooms.

III

You tossed a blanket from the bed,
You lay upon your back, and waited;
You dozed, and watched the night revealing
The thousand sordid images
Of which your soul was constituted;
They flickered against the ceiling.
And when all the world came back
And the light crept up between the shutters
And you heard the sparrows in the gutters,
You had such a vision of the street
As the street hardly understands;
Sitting along the bed's edge, where
You curled the papers from your hair,
Or clasped the yellow soles of feet
In the palms of both soiled hands.

IV

His soul stretched tight across the skies
That fade behind a city block,
Or trampled by insistent feet
At four and five and six o'clock;
And short square fingers stuffing pipes,
And evening newspapers, and eyes
Assured of certain certainties,
The conscience of a blackened street
Impatient to assume the world.

I am moved by fancies that are curled
Around these images, and cling:
The notion of some infinitely gentle
Infinitely suffering thing.

Wipe your hand across your mouth, and laugh;
The worlds revolve like ancient women
Gathering fuel in vacant lots.

MORNING AT THE WINDOW

They are rattling breakfast plates in basement kitchens
And along the trampled edges of the street
I am aware of the damp souls of housemaids
Sprouting despondently at area gates.

The brown waves of fog toss up to me
Twisted faces from the bottom of the street,
And tear from a passer-by with muddy skirts
An aimless smile that hovers in the air
And vanishes along the level of the roofs.

WIND AND SILVER

Greatly shining,
The Autumn moon floats in the thin sky;
And the fish-ponds shake their backs and
    flash their dragon scales
As she passes over them.

A DECADE

When you came, you were like red wine and honey,
And the taste of you burnt my mouth with its sweetness.
Now you are like morning bread,
I hardly taste you at all for I know your savor,
But I am completely nourished.

NIGHT CLOUDS

The white mares of the moon rush along the sky
Beating their golden hoofs upon the glass Heavens;
The white mares of the moon are all standing on their hind legs
Pawing at the green porcelain doors of the remote Heavens.
Fly, Mares!
Strain your utmost,
Scatter the milky dust of stars,
Or the tiger sun will leap upon you and destroy you
With one lick of his vermilion tongue.

THE POND

Cold, wet leaves
Floating on moss-colored water,
And the croaking of frogs—
Cracked bell-notes in the twilight.

A LOVER

If I could catch the green lantern of the firefly
I could see to write you a letter.

MEDITATION

A wise man,
Watching the stars pass across the sky,
Remarked:
In the upper air the fireflies move more slowly.

A YEAR PASSES

Beyond the porcelain fence of the pleasure garden,
I hear the frogs in the blue-green ricefields;
But the sword-shaped moon
Has cut my heart in two.

A LADY

You are beautiful and faded
Like an old opera tune
Played upon a harpsichord;
Or like the sun-flooded silks
of an eighteenth-century boudoir.
In your eyes
Smolder the fallen roses of out-lived minutes,
And the perfume of your soul
Is vague and suffusing,
With the pungence of sealed spice-jars,
Your half-tones delight me,
And I grow mad with gazing
At your blent colors.

My vigor is a new-minted penny,
Which I cast at your feet.
Gather it up from the dust,
That its sparkle may amuse you.

VENUS TRANSIENS

Tell me,
Was Venus more beautiful
Than you are,
When she topped
The crinkled waves,
Drifting shoreward
On her plaited shell?
Was Botticelli's vision
Fairer than mine;
And were the painted rosebuds
He tossed his lady,
Of better worth
Than the words I blow about you
To cover your too great loveliness
As with a gauze
Of misted silver?
For me,
You stand poised
In the blue and buoyant air,
Cinctured by bright winds,
Treading the sunlight.
And the waves which precede you
Ripple and stir
The sands at my feet.

IRRADIATIONS VII

Flickering of incessant rain
On flashing pavements:
Sudden scurry of umbrellas:
Bending, recurved blossoms of the storm.

The winds came clanging and clattering
From long white highroads whipping in ribbons up summits:
They strew upon the city gusty wafts of apple-blossom,
And the rustling of innumerable translucent leaves.

Uneven tinkling, the lazy rain
Dripping from the eaves.

IRRADIATIONS X

The trees, like great jade elephants,
Chained, stamp and shake 'neath the gadflies of the breeze;
The trees lunge and plunge, unruly elephants:
The clouds are their crimson howdah-canopies,
The sunlight glints like the golden robe of a Shah.
Would I were tossed on the wrinkled backs of those trees.

LONDON EXCURSION: STATION

We descend
Into a wall of green.
Straggling shapes:
Afterwards none are seen.

I find myself
Alone.
I look back:
The city has grown.

One grey wall
Windowed, unlit.
Heavily, night
Crushes the face of it.

I go on.
My memories freeze
Like birds' cry
In hollow trees.

I go on.
Up and outright
To the hostility
Of night.

IN THE THEATRE

Darkness in the theatre:
Darkness and a multitude
Assembled in the darkness.
These who every day perform
The unique tragi-comedy
Of birth and death;
Now press upon each other,
Directing the irresistible weight of their thoughts
        to the stage.

A great broad shaft of calcium light
Cleaves, like a stroke of a sword, the darkness:
And, at the end of it,
A tiny spot which is the red nose of a comedian
Marks the goal of the spot-light and the eyes which
        people the darkness.

THE SKATERS

Black swallows swooping or gliding
In a flurry of entangled loops and curves;
The skaters skim over the frozen river.
And the grinding click of their skates as they impinge
        upon the surface,
Is like the brushing together of thin wing-tips of silver.

CHERRY ROBBERS

Under the long dark boughs, like jewels red
    In the hair of an Eastern girl
Hang strings of crimson cherries, as if had bled
    Blood-drops beneath each curl.

Under the glistening cherries, with folded wings
    Three dead birds lie:
Pale-breasted throstles and a blackbird, robberlings
    Stained with red dye.

Against the haystack a girl stands laughing at me,
    Cherries hung round her ears.
Offers me her scarlet fruit: I will see
    If she has any tears.

A WHITE BLOSSOM

A tiny moon as small and white as a single jasmine flower
Leans all alone above my window, on night's wintry bower
Liquid as lime-tree blossom, soft as brilliant water or rain
She shines, the first white love of my youth, passionless
            and in vain.

GREEN

The dawn was apple-green,
    The sky was green wine held up in the sun,
The moon was a golden petal between.

She opened her eyes, and green
    They shone, clear like flowers undone
For the first time, now for the first time seen.

ON THE BALCONY

In front of the somber mountains, a faint, lost ribbon of rainbow;
And between us and it, the thunder;
And down below in the green wheat, the laborers
Stand like dark stumps, still in the green wheat.

You are near to me, and your naked feet in their sandals,
And through the scent of the balcony's naked timber
I distinguish the scent of your hair: so now the limber
Lightning falls from heaven.

Adown the pale-green glacier river floats
A dark boat through the gloom—and whither?
The thunder roars. But still we have each other!
The naked lightnings in the heavens dither
And disappear—what have we but each other?
The boat has gone.

TREES IN THE GARDEN

Ah in the thunder air
how still the trees are!

And the lime-tree, lovely and tall, every leaf silent
hardly looses even a last breath of perfume.

And the ghostly, creamy colored little trees of leaves
white, ivory white among the rambling greens
how evanescent, variegated elder, she hesitates on the
green grass
as if, in another moment, she would disappear
with all her grace of foam!

And the larch that is only a column, it goes up too tall to see:
and the balsam-pines that are blue with the grey-blue
          blueness of things from the sea,
and the young copper beech, its leaves red-rosey at the ends
how still they are together, they stand so still
in the thunder air, all strangers to one another
as the green grass glows upwards, strangers in the garden.

THE WHITE HORSE

The youth walks up to the white horse, to put its halter on
and the horse looks at him in silence.
They are so silent they are in another world.

NOTHING TO SAVE

There is nothing to save, now all is lost,
but a tiny core of stillness in the heart
like the eye of a violet.

NOVEMBER BY THE SEA

Now in November nearer comes the sun
down the abandoned heaven.

As the dark closes round him, he draws nearer
As if for our company

At the base of the lower brain
the sun in me declines to his winter solstice
and darts a few gold rays
back to the old year's sun across the sea.

A few gold rays thickening down to red
as the sun of my soul is setting
setting fierce and undaunted, wintry
but setting, setting behind the sounding sea between my ribs,

The wide sea wins, and the dark
winter, and the great day-sun, and the sun in my soul
sinks, sinks to setting and the winter solstice
downward, they race in decline
my sun, and the great gold sun.

AWARE

Slowly the moon is rising out of the ruddy haze,
Divesting herself of her golden shift, and so
Emerging white and exquisite; and I in amaze
See in the sky before me, a woman I did not know
I loved, but there she goes, and her beauty hurts
        my heart;
I follow her down the night, begging her not to depart.

BROODING GRIEF

A yellow leaf, from the darkness
Hops like a frog before me;
Why should I start and stand still?

I was watching the woman that bore me
Stretched in the brindled darkness
Of the sick-room, rigid with will
To die: and the quick leaf tore me
Back to this rainy swill
Of leaves and lamps and the city street mingled
before me.

GLOIRE DE DIJON

When she rises in the morning
I linger to watch her;
She spreads the bath-cloth underneath the window
Glistening white on the shoulders,
While down her sides the mellow
Golden shadow glows as
She stoops to the sponge, and her swung breasts
Sway like full-blown yellow
Gloire de Dijon roses.

She drips herself with water, and her shoulders
Glisten as silver, they crumple up
Like wet and falling roses, and I listen
For the sluicing of their rain-disheveled petals,
In the window full of sunlight
Concentrates her golden shadow
Fold on fold, until it glows as
Mellow as the glory roses.

AUTUMN RAIN

The plane leaves
fall black and wet
on the lawn;

the cloud sheaves
in heaven's fields set
droop and are drawn

in falling seeds of rain;
the seed of heaven
on my face

falling—I hear again
like echoes even
that softly pace

heaven's muffled floor,
the winds that tread . . .
out all the grain

of tears, the store
harvested
in the sheaves of pain

caught up aloft:
the sheaves of dead
men that are slain

now winnowed soft
on the floor of heaven;
manna invisible

of all the pain
here to us given;
finely divisible
falling as rain.

SWAN

Far-off
at the core of space
at the quick
of time
beats
and goes still
the great swan upon the waters of all endings
the swan within vast chaos, within
the electron.

For us
no longer he swims calmly
nor clacks across the forces furrowing a great gay trail
of happy energy,
nor is he nesting passive upon the atoms,
nor flying north desolative icewards
to the sleep of ice,
nor feeding in the marshes,
nor honking horn-like into the twilight.—

But he stoops, now
in the dark
upon us;
he is treading our women
and we men are put out
as the vast white bird
furrows our featherless women
with unknown shocks
and stamps his black marsh-feet on their white and marshy flesh.

FOG

The fog comes on
little cat feet.

It sits looking over
harbor and city
on silent haunches
and then moves on.

LOST

Desolate and lone
All night long on the lake
Where fog trails and mist creeps,
The whistle of a boat
Calls and cries unendingly,
Like some lost child
In tears and trouble
Hunting the harbor's breast
And the harbor's eyes.

MONOTONE

   The monotone of the rain is beautiful,
And the sudden rise and slow relapse
Of the long multitudinous rain.

   The sun on the hills is beautiful,
Or a captured sunset sea-flung,
Bannered with fire and gold.

   A face I know is beautiful—
With fire and gold of sky and sea,
And the peace of long warm rain.

THE HARBOR

Passing through huddled and ugly walls,
By doorways where women haggard
Looked from their hunger-deep eyes,
Haunted with shadows of hunger-hands,
Out from the huddled and ugly walls,
I came sudden, at the city's edge,
On a blue burst of lake,
Long lake waves breaking under the sun
On a spray-flung curve of shore;
And a fluttering storm of gulls,
Masses of great gray wings
And flying white bellies
Veering and wheeling free in the open.

NOCTURNE IN A DESERTED BRICKYARD

Stuff of the moon
Runs on the lapping sand
Out to the longest shadows.
Under the curving willows,
And round the creep of the wave line,
Fluxions of yellow and dusk on the waters
Make a wide dreaming pansy of an old pond in the night.

UNDER THE HARVEST MOON

Under the harvest moon,
When the soft silver
Drips shimmering
Over the garden nights,
Death, the gray mocker,
Comes and whispers to you
As a beautiful friend
Who remembers.

Under the summer roses
When the flagrant crimson
Lurks in the dusk
Of the wild red leaves,
Love, with little hands,
Comes and touches you
With a thousand memories,
And asks you
Beautiful, unanswerable questions.

TO A CHAMELEON

Hid by the august foliage and fruit
   of the grape-vine
   twine
      your anatomy
         round the pruned and polished stem,
            Chameleon.
            Fire laid upon
         an emerald as long as
      the Dark King's massy
   one,
could not snap the spectrum up for food
   as you have done.

TO A STEAM ROLLER

The illustration
is nothing to you without the application.
   You lack half wit. You crush all the particles down
      into close conformity, and then walk back and forth
         on them.

Sparkling chips of rock
are crushed down to the level of the parent block.
   Were not "impersonal judgment in aesthetic
      matters, a metaphysical impossibility," you

might fairly achieve
it. As for butterflies, I can hardly conceive
   of one's attending upon you, but to question
      the congruence of the complement is vain, if it exists.

THE FISH

wade
through black jade.
  Of the crow-blue mussel-shells, one keeps
  adjusting the ash-heaps;
    opening and shutting itself like

an
injured fan.
  The barnacles which encrust the side
  of the wave, cannot hide
    there for the submerged shafts of the

sun,
split, like spun
  glass, move themselves with spotlight swiftness
  into the crevices—
    in and out, illuminating

the
turquoise sea
  of bodies. The water drives a wedge
  of iron through the iron edge
    of the cliff; whereupon the stars,

pink
rice-grains, ink-
  bespattered jelly-fish, crabs like green
  lilies, and submarine
    toadstools, slide each on the other.

All
external
  marks of abuse are present on this
  defiant edifice—
    all the physical features of

ac-
cident—lack
　　of cornice, dynamite grooves, burns, and
　　hatchet strokes, these things stand
　　　　out on it; the chasm-side is

dead.
Repeated
　　evidence has proved that it can live
　　on what can not revive
　　　　its youth. The sea grows old in it.

NO SWAN SO FINE

"No water so still as the
    dead fountains of Versailles." No swan,
with swart blind look askance
and gondoliering legs, so fine
    as the chintz china one with fawn-
brown eyes and toothed gold
collar on to show whose bird it was.

Lodged in the Louis Fifteenth
    candelabrum-tree of cockscomb-
tinted buttons, dahlias,
sea-urchins, and everlastings,
    it perches on the branching foam
of polished sculptured
flowers—at ease and tall. The king is dead.

A TALISMAN

Under a splintered mast,
torn from the ship and cast
        near her hull,

a stumbling shepherd found
embedded in the ground
        a sea-gull

of lapis lazuli,
a scarab of the sea,
        with wings spread—

curling its coral feet,
parting its beak to greet
        men long dead.

NUANCES OF A THEME BY WILLIAMS

It's a strange courage you
give me, ancient star.

Shine alone in the sunrise
toward which you lend no part!

I

Shine alone, shine nakedly, shine like bronze,
That reflects neither my face nor any inner part
of my being, shine like fire, that mirrors nothing.

II

Lend no part to any humanity that suffuses
you in its own light.
Be not chimera of morning,
Half-man, half-star.
Be not an intelligence,
Like a widow's bird
Or an old horse.

VALLEY CANDLE

My candle burned alone in an immense valley.
Beams of the huge night converged upon it,
Until the wind blew.
Then beams of the huge night
Converged upon its image,
Until the wind blew.

DISILLUSIONMENT OF TEN O'CLOCK

The houses are haunted
By white night-gowns.
None are green,
Or purple with green rings,
Or green with yellow rings,
Or yellow with blue rings.
None of them are strange,
With socks of lace
And beaded ceintures.
People are not going
To dream of baboons and periwinkles.
Only, here and there, an old sailor,
Drunk and asleep in his boots,
Catches tigers
In red weather.

DOMINATION OF BLACK

At night, by the fire,
The colors of the bushes
And of the fallen leaves,
Repeating themselves,
Turned in the room,
Like the leaves themselves
Turning in the wind.
Yes: but the color of the heavy hemlocks
Came striding.
And I remembered the cry of the peacocks.

The colors of their tails
Were like the leaves themselves
Turning in the wind,
In the twilight wind.
They swept over the room,
just as they flew from the boughs of the
          hemlocks
Down to the ground.
I heard them cry—the peacocks.
Was it a cry against the twilight
Or against the leaves themselves
Turning in the wind,
Turning as the flames
Turned in the fire,
Turning as the tails of the peacocks
Turned in the loud fire,
Loud as the hemlocks
Full of the cry of the peacocks?
Or was it a cry against the hemlocks?

Out of the window,
I saw how the planets gathered
Like the leaves themselves
Turning in the wind.
I saw how the night came,
Came striding like the color of the heavy hemlocks
I felt afraid.
And I remembered the cry of the peacocks.

FAREWELL WITHOUT A GUITAR

Spring's bright paradise has come to this.
Now the thousand-leaved green falls to the ground.
Farewell, my days.

The thousand-leaved red
Comes to this thunder of light
At its autumnal terminal—

A Spanish storm,
A wide, still Aragonese,
In which the horse walks home without a rider,

Head down. The reflections and repetitions,
The blows and buffets of fresh senses
Of the rider that was,

Are a final construction,
Like glass and sun, of male reality
And of that other and her desire.

THIRTEEN WAYS OF LOOKING AT A BLACKBIRD

I

Among twenty snowy mountains,
The only moving thing
Was the eye of the blackbird.

II

I was of three minds,
Like a tree
In which there are three blackbirds.

III

The blackbird whirled in the autumn winds.
It was a small part of the pantomime.

IV

A man and a woman
Are one.
A man and a woman and a blackbird
Are one.

V

I do not know which to prefer,
The beauty of inflections
Or the beauty of innuendoes,
The blackbird whistling
Or just after.

VI

Icicles filled the long window
With barbaric glass.
The shadow of the blackbird
Crossed it, to and fro.
The mood
Traced in the shadow
An undecipherable cause.

VII

O thin men of Haddam,
Why do you imagine golden birds?
Do you not see how the blackbird
Walks around the feet
Of the women about you?

VIII

I know noble accents
And lucid, inescapable rhythms;
But I know, too,
That the blackbird is involved
In what I know.

IX

When the blackbird flew out of sight,
It marked the edge
Of one of many circles.

X

At the sight of blackbirds
Flying in a green light,
Even the bawds of euphony
Would cry out sharply.

XI

He rode over Connecticut
In a glass coach.
Once, a fear pierced him,
In that he mistook
The shadow of his equipage
For blackbirds.

XII

The river is moving.
The blackbird must be flying.

XIII

It was evening all afternoon.
It was snowing
And it was going to snow.
The blackbird sat
In the cedar-limbs.

STUDY OF TWO PEARS

I

Opusculum paedagogum.[1]
The pears are not viols,
Nudes or bottles.
They resemble nothing else.

II

They are yellow forms
Composed of curves
Bulging toward the base.
They are touched red.

III

They are not flat surfaces
Having curved outlines.
They are round
Tapering toward the top.

IV

In the way they are modeled
There are bits of blue.
A hard dry leaf hangs
From the stem.

V

The yellow glistens.
It glistens with various yellows,
Citrons, oranges and greens
Flowering over the skin.

VI

The shadows of the pears
Are blobs on the green cloth.
The pears are not seen
As the observer wills.

[1] Latin phrase meaning "little teaching work".

ANECDOTE OF THE JAR

I placed a jar in Tennessee,
And round it was, upon a hill.
It made the slovenly wilderness
Surround that hill.

The wilderness rose up to it,
And sprawled around, no longer wild.
The jar was round upon the ground
And tall and of a port in air.

It took dominion everywhere.
The jar was grey and bare.
It did not give of bird or bush
Like nothing else in Tennessee.

CURFEW

Like a faun my head uplifted
In delicate mists:

And breaking on my soul
Tremulous waves that beat and cling
To yellow leaves and dark green hills:

Bells in the autumn evening.

NIGHT

The dark steep roofs chisel
The infinity of the sky:

But the white moonlight gables
Resemble
Still hands at prayer.

THE WARNING

Just now,
Out of the strange
Still dusk ... as strange, as still ...
A white moth flew. Why am I grown
So cold?

NIAGARA
Seen on a Night in November

How frail
Above the bulk
Of crashing water hangs,
Autumnal, evanescent, wan,
The moon.

TRIAD

These be
Three silent things:
The falling snow . . . the hour
Before the dawn . . . the mouth of one
Just dead.

NOVEMBER NIGHT

Listen. . .
With faint dry sound,
Like steps of passing ghosts,
The leaves, frost-crisp'd, break from the trees
And fall.

MIDNIGHT

Midnight. The air is still,
And yet there seems to be a sound
Brooding in it, tearing. I hear it
With all my quivering body
But not with my ears.
Suddenly it bursts—muffled, hoarse, detached
From any earthly object.
It is spring
Charging through the night.

IMPRESSION V

stinging
gold swarms
upon the spires
silver

     chants the litanies the
great bells are ringing with rose
the lewd fat bells
          and a tall

wind
is dragging
the
sea

with

dream

-S

BUFFALO BILL'S

Buffalo Bill's
defunct
           who used to
           ride a watersmooth-silver
                                  stallion
and break onetwothreefourfive pigeonsjustlikethat

                                             Jesus

he was a handsome man
                          and what I want to know is
how do you like your blueeyed boy
Mister Death

1(a
          l(a

          le
          af
          fa

          ll

          s)
          one
          l

          iness

ARS POETICA

A poem should be palpable and mute
As a globed fruit

Dumb
As old medallions to the thumb

Silent as the sleeve-worn stone
Of casement ledges where the moss has grown—

A poem should be wordless
As the flight of birds

A poem should be motionless in time
As the moon climbs

Leaving, as the moon releases
Twig by twig the night-entangled trees,

Leaving, as the moon behind the winter leaves,
Memory by memory the mind—

A poem should be motionless in time
As the moon climbs

A poem should be equal to:
Not true

For all the history of grief
An empty doorway and a maple leaf

For love
The leaning grasses and two lights above the sea—

A poem should not mean
But be.

PRIMARY SOURCES

Books

Des Imagistes: An Anthology. New York; Albert & Charles Boni, 1914.
Some Imagist Poets, 3 vols. Boston: Houghton Mifflin, 1915, 1916, 1917.
Aldington, Richard. *Images.* London: The Egoist, (C. 1915). *Collected Poems,*
    1915-1923. London: Allen & Unwin, 1933.
Crapsey, Adelaide. *Verse.* New York: Alfred A. Knopf, 1915.
Cummings, E. E. *Complete Poems 1913-62.* New York: Harcourt, Brace,
    Jovanovich, 1972.
Eliot, T. S. *Collected Poems,* 1909-35. New York: Harcourt, Brace, 1936.
Fletcher, John Gould. *Irradiations.* Boston: Houghton Mifflin, 1915.
H.D. (Hilda Doolittle). *Collected Poems, 1912-1944.* Edited by Louis Martz.
    New York: New Directions, 1925, 1944, 1982. *Selected Poems of H.D.* New
    York: Grove Press, 1957.
Hulme, T. E. *Speculations.* Edited by Herbert Read. New York: Harcourt
    Brace, 1924. *Further Speculations.* Edited by Sam Hynes. Minneapolis:
    University of Minnesota Press,1955.
Jones, Alun. *The Life and Opinions of T. E. Hulme.* Boston: Beacon Press,
    1960.
D. H. Lawrence. *The Complete Poems of D.H. Lawrence.* Edited by Vivian de
    Sola Pinto & Warren Roberts. 2 vols. New York: Viking Press, 1964.
Lowell, Amy. *The Complete Poetical Works of Amy Lowell.* Boston: Houghton
    Mifflin, 1955.
Moore, Marianne. *The Complete Poems of Marianne Moore.* New York:
    Viking, 1981.
Pound, Ezra. *Personae: The Shorter Poems.* Revised edition by Lea
    Baechler & A. Walton Litz. New York: New Directions, 1926, 1935, 1971.
Read, Herbert. *Collected Poems.* London: Faber & Faber, 1946.
Stevens, Wallace. *Collected Poems,* New York: Alfred A. Knopf, 1955. *Opus
    Posthumous,* New York: Alfred A. Knopf, 1957.
Williams, William Carlos. *The Collected Poems of William Carlos
    Williams.*Vol. I, 1909-1939, Edited by A. Walton Litz & Christopher
    MacGowan. Vol. II, 1939-1962, Edited by Christopher MacGowan. New
    York: New Directions, 1986, 1988.

Magazines

The Egoist. London. Vols. I-VI (1914-19). (Special Imagist Number: May 1,
    1915).
The Little Review. Chicago, New York, Paris. Vols. I-VIII (1914-29).
Poetry. Chicago. Vols. 1- (1912-

SECONDARY SOURCES

Books

Aldington, Richard. *Life for Life's Sake.* New York: Viking Press, 1941.

Chasna, Edmund S. de. *John Gould Fletcher and Imagism.* Columbia: University of Missouri Press, 1978.

Coffman, Stanley K. *Imagism, A Chapter for the History of Modern Poetry.* Norman, Oklahoma: University of Oklahoma Press, 1951.

Eliot, T. S. Ezra Pound. *His Metric and Poetry.* New York: Alfred A. Knopf, 1917.

Fletcher, John Gould. *Life is My Song.* New York: Farrar & Rinehart. 1937.

Gage, John T. *In the Arresting Eye: The Rhetoric of Imagism.* Baton Rouge: Louisiana State University Press, 1981.

Gould, Jean. *Amy: The World of Amy Lowell and the Imagist Movement.* New York: Dodd, Mead, 1975.

Grover, Philip, ed. *Ezra Pound: The London Years, 1908-1920.* New York: AMS Press, 1978.

Harmer, J.B. *Victory in Limbo: Imagism, 1908-1917.* London: Secker and Warburg, 1975.

Homage to Imagism. Edited by William Pratt and Robert Richardson. New York: AMS Press, 1991.

Hough, Graham. *Reflections on a Literary Revolution.* Washington: Catholic University Press, 1960.

Hughes, Glenn. *Imagism and the Imagists: A Study in Modern Poetry.* Stanford: Stanford University Press, 1931.

Jones, Peter. *Imagist Poetry.* London: Pengin Books, 1972.

Kermode, Frank. *Romantic Image.* London: Routledge & Kegan Paul, 1957.

Monroe, Harriet. *A Poet's Life.* New York: The Macmillan Co., 1938.

Pound, Ezra. *The Letters of Ezra Pound, 1907-41.* Edited by D. D. Paige, New York: Harcourt, Brace, 1950. *The Literary Essays of Ezra Pound.* Ed. by T. S. Eliot. New York: New Directions, 1954.

Qian, Zhaoming. Orientalism and Modernism: The Legacy of China in Pound and Williams. Durham & London: Duke University Press, 1995.

Smith, William Jay. *The Spectra Hoax.* Ashland, Oregon: Story Line Press, 2000.

Stead, C.K. *The New Poetic: Yeats to Eliot.* London: Penguin Books, 1964.

Taupin, Renè. *The Influence of French Symbolism on Modern American Poetry.* Translated by William Pratt and Anne Rich Pratt. Edited, with introductory and concluding essays, by William Pratt. New York: AMS Press, 1985.

Williams, William Carlos. *Autobiography.* New York: Random House, 1951. *Selected Letters.* New York: McDowell, Obolensky, 1957.

Essays, Articles, Chapters in Books

Blackmur, R. P. "Lord Tennyson's Scissors: 1912-1950" in *Form and Value in Modern Poetry.* New York: Doubleday Anchor Books, 1957. Pages 369-88.

Brooks, Cleanth, Lewis, R.W.B. & Warren, Robert Penn, editors. *American Literature: The Makers and the Making. Volume II.* Introductory Essay "From Imagism to Symbolism," New York: St. Martins Press, 1973. Pages 2043-63.

Cambon, Glauco. "Revolution and Tradition," *Poetry,* C (April, 1962). Pages 50-54.

Eliot, T.S. "American Literature and the American Language," in *To Criticize the Critic.* New York: Farrar, Straus & Giroux, 1965. Pages 43-60.

Flint, F. S. "The History of Imagism," Egoist, 11 (May 1, 1915), Pages 70-71.

___. "Imagisme," *Poetry,* I (January, 1913), Pages 198-200.

Geiger, Don. "Imagism: New Poetry Forty Years Later," *Prairie Schooner,* XXX (1956), Pages 139-47.

"Imagism" in *A Handbook to Literature.* Edited by C. Hugh Holman & William Harmon. New York: Macmillan, 1986. Page 251.

Isaac , J. "The Coming of the Image," in *The Background of Modern Poetry.* New York: Dutton Paperbacks, 1952. Pages 34-51.

Jarrell, Randall, "Introduction" to *Selected Poems of W. C. Williams.* New York: New Directions, 1949. Pages ix-xix.

Jones, Alun R. "Notes Toward a History of Imagism." *South Atlantic Quarterly*, LX (Summer, 1961). Pages 262-85.

Kenner, Hugh. "Why Imagism?" in *The Poetry of Ezra Pound*, Norfolk, Conn.: New Directions, n.d. (1950). Pages 56-61.

Matthiessen, F. 0. "Introduction" to *The Oxford Book of American Verse.* New York: Oxford University Press, 1950. Pages ix-xxxiii.

Miner, Earl. "Pound, Haiku, and the Image," *Hudson Review,* IX (Winter, 1957). Pages 570-84.

Pound, Ezra. "Vorticism," *Fortnightly Review,* XCVI, n.s. (September 1, 1914). Pages 461-71. "A Retrospect." First published in *Pavannes and Divisions* (1918). Reprinted in *The Literary Essays of Ezra Pound.* Pages 3-14.

Pratt, William. "Ezra Pound and the Image" and "The Image in the Cantos," in *Singing the Chaos: Madness and Wisdom in Modern Poetry.* Columbia: University of Missouri Press, 1996. Pages 126-46.

Read, Herbert, "The Image in Modern English Poetry," and "Ezra Pound," in *The Tenth Muse.* London: Routledge & Kegan Paul, 1957. Pages 117-38, 260-75.

Spender, Stephen. "The Seminal Image" in *The Struggle of the Modern.* Berkeley: University of California Press, 1963. Pages 110-15.

Stock, Noel. "Imagism, 1912/1914," in *The Life of Ezra Pound* New York: Pantheon Books (Random House), 1970. Pages 115-147.

Printed by CDS Documentation
2661 S. Pacific Hwy.
Medford, OR 97501
541.773.7575